LAISSEZ FAIRE'S

BIG BOOK OF

FREE

Over 127 Ways to Get What You Want & Need For Free – Or For Pennies On The Dollar

LAISSEZ FAIRE'S

BIG BOOK OF

FREE

Over 127 Ways to Get What You Want & Need For Free – Or For Pennies On The Dollar

 Laissez Faire Books

ISBN: 978-1-6212913-0-5 (print)

18 17 16 15 14   1 2 3 4 5 6 7

Published by Laissez Faire Books, 808 St. Paul Street, Baltimore, Maryland
www.lfb.org

Cover Design: Mena Fusco
Layout Design: Andre Cawley

Table of Contents

Introduction

The book you hold in your hands is chock-full of extremely powerful tricks, hacks and insider secrets. Inside, you'll discover over 127 simple ways to get what you want or need — while spending far less than everyone else does.

We've spent countless hours of independent research to find the best, simplest, and fastest ways to get what you want for free... or for pennies on the dollar.

Do you want to know how to get paid to play golf? Enroll in Ivy League Courses for free? Find beautiful places to stay anywhere in the world for free? Do you want to get a free car? Free gold? A free house? Start your own home business for $0 down and keep it running with no overhead? It's all here.

But *Laissez Faire's Big Book of Free* is about more than just getting free stuff. It's about raising your standard of living without sacrificing all your time, energy, and peace of mind. Sure, there might be some work involved. With any radical change in your life, a little work is to be expected. But with the help of *Laissez Faire's Book of Free*, you'll be able to...finally...live on your own terms.

Your journey to a better life begins today. Enjoy.

Sincerely,

The Laissez Faire Club Research Team

Chapter One: Travel

How to Fly For Free
(or for Pennies On The Dollar)

This secret alone is good for up to $5,000 in free airfare per year (possibly more), plus free first-class upgrades.

It all comes down to one thing: **Using credit cards wisely**.

If you don't use a rewards credit card for every single thing you buy, now's the time to start. Credit card companies are down on one knee *begging* for your attention, and they're willing to give you lots of really nice perks for your patronage. All that's required is that you have decent credit.

Yes, we'll cover other powerful methods for free travel in this book aside from just gathering credit card points. But earning free travel with reward credit cards should be your first step. It's easy, legitimate, and extremely profitable. It's how elite travelers hitch rides all across the world for free.

Here's how you do it...

First, always be on the lookout and take advantage of frequent flier mile promotions. For example, at the time of writing, **Chase** is shelling out 40,000 bonus miles just for signing up for their **Sapphire** card.

That's good for $750 toward your next plane ticket. Where could you go **today** if you had $750 in free airfare?

Sign up for a few of these offers every two months or so and you'll easily rack up thousands of dollars in free travel in just one year.

Visit this link for a list of the best current travel credit card offers: www.hackmytrip.com/best-travel-credit-cards/

Wait a minute... won't signing up for this many cards hurt my credit? Not necessarily. I'll tell you why in a moment.

First, here's more about how these bonuses work...

Credit Card Bonus (And The Catch)

If you're American, count yourself lucky that you live in a country where credit card issuers compete so hard for your business. They are falling over themselves to offer you the most valuable sign-on bonuses.

As mentioned, with the **Chase Sapphire** card you can earn 40,000 points (good for up to $750 in travel) when you sign up.

The only catch is (you knew there had to be one, right?) **you must spend at least $3,000 on the card in three months**.

But that doesn't mean you have to put yourself in debt just to get the points. That would defeat the purpose. I'm going to show you how to meet the minimum without spending a penny more than you normally would.

Push It to the Limit

Getting to that $3,000 minimum in 90 days is simple.

Your first step is to buy everything you normally purchase on the card. Food, gas, and even your taxes can be paid through your credit card.

Every time you buy something and don't use your rewards card, you're missing out on an opportunity for FREE travel.

If you can't reach the limit with just your normal expenses, you could choose to pay your mortgage or rent with your credit card (for a small fee) at WilliamPaid.

WilliamPaid: www.williampaid.com

But before you do that, consider this little-known secret...

One Insider Secret to Meet the Minimum

There are many sneaky (and 100% legal) ways to meet the minimum without overspending. So let's say your monthly expenses are low and spending $3,000 in 90 days is impossible.

Don't worry.

One great trick, while it lasts, is to use Amazon's new payment system. Upon writing, **Amazon Payments** allows users to send up to $1,000 from a credit card to anyone in the world (who also has Amazon Payments), absolutely free.

For this trick, you're going to need a friend.

First, you and a friend each sign up for Amazon Payments. You add your credit card to your account and send him or her $1,000. Of course, make sure it's someone you trust.

Your friend then writes you a check for that amount, you deposit it in the bank, and pay off the credit card. And now you've knocked out $1,000 you would've had to spend on the card. You can do this month after month, too. Absolutely free.

It really is as easy as that.

This is a great way to meet the minimum spend if your regular expenses won't cover it. If you want to learn more ways to meet credit card minimums, check out this website:

www.thepointsguy.com/2014/03/top-10-ways-to-meet-credit-card-bonus-minimum-spending-requirements/

How it Works/Credit Score Questions

After you sign up for your first card and see all the money credit card companies are just giving away, you'll be hooked.

And that's where the rubber meets the road: As soon as you meet the minimum on one card, simply sign up for the next best offer you can find. Then use the tricks I told you about to meet the minimums as quickly as possible.

For example, let's say your MasterCard requires you to spend $3,000 in the first three months of having the card. You use this card for all of your expenses and pay it off in full each month. You also use the **Amazon Payments** trick I told you about for $1,000.

Let's say you meet the requirement in two months. That's when you sign up for a new card with another great bonus offer and repeat the process.

Keep going and you'll have enough points to travel wherever you want in a few short months. On top of all the bonus points you'll rack up, each dollar you spend will earn you points toward travelling. In all, you could rack up $5,000 worth of free airfare in less than a year... maybe much more.

[NOTE: Many of these cards do have an annual fee. I recommend you choose those cards that waive the first year free. Hold onto those cards as long as you can go without paying an annual fee. To learn how to get your fee waived year after year, check out **To Beat the Annual Fee, Do This in Chapter Twelve.***]*

OK, now to the elephant in the room.

Won't this hurt my credit score? The truth? Yes and no.

At first, your credit score will take a small hit (about three to five points). That's why you should only inquire about credit cards you really want: Those with attractive sign-on bonuses.

But here's the caveat: In the long run, it will HELP your credit.

See, the idea that opening up several cards will kill your credit score simply isn't true. A large chunk of your credit score determined by your credit-to-debt ratio. The lower it is, the better. So opening up more lines of credit (while keeping a low amount of debt) will inevitably raise your credit rating in the long run.

This is, of course, a simplistic explanation. If you want a detailed explanation, follow this link:

How Opening and Closing Credit Cards Affects Your Credit Score: www.mymoneyblog.com/how-opening-and-closing-credit-card-accounts-affects-your-credit-score.html

Here's the distilled version: As long as you're paying off the credit card in full (which you should be because you're only spending it on normal expenses), your score won't suffer. In fact, all of this will HELP your credit score!

[NOTE: Don't miss a payment, though! A late payment on your credit report could cut more than 100 points off your credit score.]

At the time of writing, the three best cards are three **Chase** cards: **Sapphire**, **Ink Bold**, and **Ink Plus**. You'll earn 40,000, 50,000 and 50,000 points (enough for over $2,000 in airfare) respectively on these cards, and there are no foreign transaction fees. Also, for every dollar you spend on any business expenses involving Internet, telecommunications, and office supply stores on your Bold or Ink cards, **you'll also earn five times that in points, up to $50,000 a year**.

Below is a great list of the best travel credit card offers that are regularly updated.

www.hackmytrip.com/best-travel-credit-cards/

Expand your reach: Hotels also compete to give out the best sign-up bonuses on their branded cards. Here's a quick rundown of the best hotel cards:

www.thesimpledollar.com/best-hotel-credit-cards/

[NOTE: All bonus points can also be redeemed for cash or gift cards. As a general rule, every 10,000 points you earn are worth $100. So for example, a 40,000 point sign-on bonus will net you $400.]

Get Bumped

Want a way to get your ticket near-free without the use of credit cards?

This technique is sneaky and will take a bit of finesse and time. Here's how it works...

In an effort to maximize revenue, every single airline in the world has one common practice: They all overbook popular flights. For savvy flyers, this creates a unique opportunity to hack the system.

See, when a plane is oversold, some travelers will volunteer to take a later flight. In exchange, they'll receive hundreds of dollars in compensation. The key to getting bumped is to book flights you know will be oversold. Just make sure you don't check your luggage and get there early. You want to be first on the list of volunteers when the gate agents arrive, and they prefer someone who is packing light.

The flights most likely to be overbooked are routes frequented by business travelers. For that reason, **most occur on Monday mornings or between 4 p.m. and 7 p.m. on weekdays**.

Here are more flight times likely to be overbooked...

- Departures after noon on Fridays or Sunday evenings
- Pre- and post-holiday flights
- And popular routes during tourist season.

Before you use this trick, remember this: You're not guaranteed to get bumped, so don't count on it completely. This trick is useful when you have some time on your hands and don't mind what happens either way.

All you do is show up a little early, inform the clerk at your gate that you're willing to get bumped if they're overbooked, and wait it out.

Here are some examples of what's possible if you pull it off, taken from some online sources...

> *"Once, I bumped my flight and got a free round-trip pass to anywhere in the U.S.... the makeup flight they scheduled me on was only 20 minutes later, and it was a direct flight, instead of a one-stop. I made it two hours earlier than I was originally planning."*

> — Alias **PiNPOiNT** on *Lifehacker.com*

> *"My wife and I were flying back from visiting her sister in Seattle several years ago. We had a connecting flight out of Memphis, which ended up being overbooked/ overweight, and they offered free round-trip tickets to anywhere in the lower 48, Canada, Mexico, or the Caribbean, or a $300 travel voucher, to any volunteers."*

> — Alias **gbfreak** on *Lifehacker.com*

BRIGHT SIDE: Even if it fails and you do get on the plane, there is a bright side. Since you volunteered to take the hit, you're more likely to get moved up to first-class for free just for volunteering before anyone else.

You should always be polite when dealing with airport staff. They hold the power to make your flight as comfortable as possible.

They deal with rude people every single day. If you're polite, it's refreshing and they'll want to be nice to you too.

Which brings me to our next secret...

Know When to Complain

When an airline experiences a service failure, many customers become rude and impatient. But you should ALWAYS stay calm and polite whenever this happens.

If you play your cards right, you could receive generous compensation from your travel provider and/or the travel clerks themselves.

If you take the time to write a brief, polite email to your travel provider, and be empathetic to your travel clerks, you'll up your chances of receiving vouchers and frequent flier miles for your troubles.

Being nice pays off.

If you don't hear back via email within a few days, simply call up customer relations about the flight. More often than not, if a problem was reported about the flight you were on, you'll receive some form of compensation.

Get a Refund

Most don't know this, but if you've already bought a ticket and find the same flight cheaper elsewhere, most ticket dealers, and even some airlines, will refund the difference.

In fact, online travel company **Orbitz** announced in 2013 that they will automatically refund customers if the airfare drops after they've bought the ticket.

Orbitz: www.orbitz.com

Expedia has a lowest-price guaranteed policy on flights, hotels, vacation packages, rental cars, and more. Find a better deal within 24 hours of booking and they'll refund the difference plus give you a travel coupon worth $50.

Expedia: www.expedia.com

Priceline has the same deal as Expedia.

Priceline: www.priceline.com

American Airlines, Alaska Air, United Airlines, Delta, and **Frontier Airlines** all provide lowest-price guarantees. And if you find a lower price, most will not only refund the difference, they'll also give you travel certificates worth up to $100 in airfare.

American Airlines:
www.aa.com/guarantee
Alaska Air:
www.alaskaair.com/content/deals/special-offers/price-guarantee.aspx
United Airlines:
www.united.com
Delta Airlines:
www.delta.com/content/www/en_US/traveling-with-us/planning-a-trip/booking-information/online-booking/best-fare-guarantee.html
Frontier Airlines:
www.flyfrontier.com/customer-service/best-fare-guarantee

Hire Your Own Negotiator

If you prefer, a company called **Yapta** will haggle with the airline or travel company on your behalf for a small percentage of your savings.

Yapta: www.yapta.com

Skip Past Airline Security In Seconds

Use the following program and get whisked past security at the airport. Once enrolled, you'll be able to keep your shoes, belt, and jacket on every time you travel.

[Note: Before we begin, you should know that this program is not free. It involves a one-time fee of $85. We included it in this book because if you're a frequent traveler, we think all the time and headaches it could save you in your future travels is worth it.]

All you have to do to apply is visit the TSA's **Pre-Check** website. If you're eligible, you'll be able to go through a *much* quicker "VIP" line and avoid the pat-downs and invasive scanners.

Just so you're aware, the TSA will require documentation of your fingerprints to be taken at the airport before you can enter this program.

TSA Pre-Check:

www.tsa.gov/tsa-precheck/application-program

How to Get Free Accomodation Anywhere in the World

If you've ever done any extensive traveling, you know that accom-modation is always one of the biggest money suckers.

So what if you could strike accommodation off your expense list altogether?

The more money you save on where you sleep, the more time you'll be able to travel, the more places you'll see, and the more financially sustainable your travels will be.

No one knows this better than Nora Dunn.

In 2006, Nora sold her financial planning practice, purged herself of all her belongings, and hopped on a plane to travel full time. Since, she's travelled through over 30 countries and five continents. And no matter where she lands, she stays for FREE. By her estimate, she's saved over $63,500 in accommodation expenses alone.

"And when accommodation is free," says Nora, "you can stay longer in the places you visit, and get a deeper culturally immer-sive experience. I have found it to be one of the most rewarding ways of seeing the world."

How does she do it? Several ways. All of which (and more) you'll learn about in this section.

Housesit

One thing she does is house (and pet) -sits whenever possible. On the Caribbean island of Grenada, for example, she spent three months in a beautiful beachfront villa and had full use of two cars.

All she had to do was watch the house while the owners were gone. Sound simple? It is.

"The concept is as simple as it sounds," Nora explains. "There are a number of websites that connect homeowners who need somebody to take care for their pets/plants/etc. in their absence with travelers who are up for the task and enthusiastic about living a slice of "local life.""

"There's some fierce competition for housesitting jobs, so you have to be quick on the draw and professional and present a good face. And you have to apply for a lot of jobs; even if you're "God's gift" to housesitting, you can expect more rejections than successful applications."

Here are Nora's 10 tips for landing the perfect house-sitting gig: www.wisebread.com/10-tips-for-landing-the-perfect-house-sitting-gig

And here's a list of house-sitting websites Nora has personally recommended:

HouseCarers: www.housecarers.com
The Caretaker Gazette: www.caretaker.org
TrustedHousesitters.com: www.trustedhousesitters.com
MindMyHouse: www.mindmyhouse.com
Housesitworld: www.housesitworld.com

Aussie House Sitters:

www.aussiehousesitters.com.au

(for Australian houses only)

House Sitters America:

www.housesittersamerica.com

(Note: To learn more about how Nora does it, check out here website at www.theprofessionalhobo.com)

Home Exchange

Here's a twist on the housesitting gig that solves one problem you may encounter: *'While I'm out taking care of someone else's house, who is going to watch mine?'*

Home Exchange is exactly what it sounds like: You exchange your home with a family from a different part of the world who wants to check out your neck of the woods. You both enjoy free accommodation in a new place, and everyone wins.

You can set the terms beforehand. Things like length of stay, who pays for what (bills and utilities), and what extra chores must be done (pets and plants).

Of course, there is an issue of security. Get to know the family before you decide to exchange homes. And many home exchange websites have measures in place to make sure you're safe.

If you're interested, check out the best websites for home exchanges below. Some of them have small fees, but they pay for themselves 20 times over on your first exchange.

HomeExchange.com: **www.homeexchange.com**

Exchangehomes.com: **www.exchangehomes.com**

International Home Exchange Network: **www.ihen.com**

International Vacation Home Exchange: **www.ivhe.com**

Intervac: intervacusa.com

InventedCity: www.invented-city.com

HomeLink: www.homelink.org

Home Base Holidays: www.homebase-hols.com

Global Home Exchange: www.4homex.com

Green Theme International Home Exchange:
www.gti-home-exchange.com

JewettStreet: www.jewettstreet.com

The Caretaker Gazette: www.caretaker.org

Seniors Home Exchange: www.seniorshomeexchange.com

Work/Trade/Volunteer

There are tons of creative opportunities to work a few hours a day in return for free stay (and oftentimes food, too.) If you're a long-term traveler, brief stints of volunteering are your best, and oftentimes most rewarding, option to keep your expenses low.

You can work a few hours a day on a farm, work at a lodge, help out at a B&B, and much more. Wherever you want to visit, there are plenty of opportunities to stay there for free and completely immerse yourself in the culture.

Help Exchange: www.helpx.net

WWOOF: www.wwoof.org

GrowFood: www.growfood.org

World Help Link: www.worldhelplink.com

PAYaway: www.payaway.co.uk

Be an Au Pair

If you're planning a long trip, why not soak in the culture completely and get paid? You can apply for an **au pair** job on nearly every continent you visit. It's a great way to learn the language and culture firsthand.

If you don't know, an au pair is simply someone who provides child care to a host family. In exchange, he or she normally gets a room and salary. The period of such programs varies; some can be as long as a year, while others last for two–three months. Au pair jobs are available in various countries, but most often seen in Europe.

Aupair World: www.aupair-world.net

Step-by-step instructions on how to become an au pair: ashleyabroad.com/2013/04/19/how-to-become-an-au-pair

Teach Abroad

Teaching abroad is one of the best and most popular ways of travelling for free. If you can speak and write, this could be your golden ticket for travelling for free.

Teaching English abroad is a rewarding way to stay in a foreign country. Oftentimes, you'll receive free room and board too. Countries like China, Vietnam, Thailand, Myanmar, and South Korea are always in search of people who can settle for a few months (or years) and teach people how to speak, read, and write in English.

Don't I need to know a foreign language? Nope. Most English teachers abroad start out not knowing the native language, and it's rarely a requirement.

Here are some terms you should know.

ESL: English as a Second Language
TEFL: Teaching English as a Foreign Language

Learn More at These Links

Teach Away: www.teachaway.com

ESL Cafe's International Job Board:
www.eslcafe.com/joblist

ESL Job Feed: www.esljobfeed.com

TotalESL: www.totalesl.com

TEFL (Teaching English as a Foreign Language):
www.tefl.com

The Council on International Educational Exchange (CIEE):
www.ciee.com

Sail On a Yacht For Free

Imagine how much longer you could travel and how much more you could do if your airfare and hotels bills were ZERO.

When traveling, you probably know, you face three major expenses.

One is transportation (airfare, bus, rental car, etc.) We've covered how to get these for free (or dirt cheap) throughout the travel section, if you choose to go these routes.

The second is accommodation. We covered how to get free accommodation in earlier sections. Please refer to the table of contents at the beginning of this book for more information.

And third is food. You'll learn several tips and tricks on how to eat cheaply (and sometimes free) within this book. But if you take advantage of this one secret... you won't need anything else to travel 100% free.

When you sail on a yacht, the first two are taken care of in one swoop. And sometimes even the third.

So why not sail on a 30-270-foot yacht for free? Yes, it's possible. Twenty-one-year-old backpackers to 80-year-old retirees are setting sail each and every day.

For example, Greg and Tiffany Norte have been doing it for years. And they've documented their journey on their blog,

CoastGuardCouple.com. What's their secret? Volunteering. And according to them, anyone can do it.

"Incidentally," they said in a recent interview, "you don't need any special qualifications or training to start as a volunteer and sail around the world for free. Since discovering this, we've been trying to get the word out. Yes, it really is as cool as it sounds. It's also ridiculously easy to do."

Every boat is different in what it needs, but all captains need the same thing: volunteers. Even if you don't have any boat-specific technical skills, an extra set of hands to share chores, cook food, and provide good company are always welcome. Many regular volunteer sailors started out with absolutely no sailing experience — now they travel across the world for free.

Offshore Passage Opportunities (OPO) is an organization that takes care of crew networking and provides crew to people who want to sail their boats or cruises to different destinations. The crewmembers of OPO travel for free, as they offer their expertise and skills to the captain and his team.

It's free to sign up as a nonmember and share your profile with sailors all around the world.

Visit their website at **www.sailopo.com** to find out more about the company and how it can help you sail the world for absolutely free.

Here are some more sites that offer these opportunities:

Find a Crew: **www.findacrew.net**
Latitude 38:
www.latitude38.com/crewlist/cruising/skipper_results.lasso
Desperate Sailors: **www.desperatesailors.com**

Exclusive interview with Greg and Tiffany: www.peanutbutternomads.com/2011/12/14/how-to-sail-around-the-world-and-live-to-tell-about-it

How they do it and extra resources: www.coastguardcouple.com/how-to-crew/races-rallies-and-sailing-schools

Other Travel Websites to Save You a Bundle

Farecast

Farecast lets you know if a hotel rate is the best deal based on past rates. They'll send you instant updates, letting you know exactly when to buy your ticket based on whether the price is rising or dropping over the next seven days.

Farecast: www.farecast.com

Kayak

It's the only site you'll need to search for discounted airfare. **Kayak** searches over 140-plus airlines and travel agencies (including all the names you're familiar with) to find the absolute best prices all over the world. It even uncovers pricing glitches. That's when an airline accidentally prices the flight too low ($7 for a trip to Hawaii, for example) and has to honor it once you purchase the ticket.

Kayak: www.kayak.com

Roomorama or Airbnb

Stay in the hottest areas in some of the biggest cities in the world for cheap. Roomorama and Airbnb is a way for you to stay in apartments all over the world for far less than you would pay at a hotel.

Whether you're going to London, Paris, Singapore or New York City, check out Roomorama or Airbnb before you go for a hotel.

Roomorama: **www.roomorama.com**

Airbnb: **www.airbnb.com**

Agoda

If you do decide on a hotel, check out Asia's premier discount service **Agoda**. They guarantee the lowest rates, and they'll let you book now and pay later. Hands down the cheapest rates I've seen online.

Agoda: **www.agoda.com**

Yapta

It stands for Your Amazing Personal Travel Assistant. And it is. **Yapta** will tell you as soon as flight prices drop, even after you purchase your tickets. Also, Yapta will let you know if a seat opens up you can use your miles on.

Yapta: **www.yapta.com**

Rome2Rio

Sometimes it's cheaper, and more gratifying, not to fly. **Rome2Rio** compiles all air, coach, ferry, mass transit, and driving options to and from any location and gives you all the cheapest options.

Rome2Rio: **www.rome2rio.com**

Get Treated Like a VIP on a Cruise

Here's how to get treated like a VIP and get free drinks on your next cruise.

First things first. Decide whether or not you're going to use a travel agent. If you are, check out these tips:

www.usatoday.com/experience/cruise/cruise-101/cruise-101-using-a-travel-agent/2127873

Before you use an agent, though, check out this trick...

Cruise the Bahamas for Less Than $200

Nearly all "preferred" cruise agencies offer last minute cruise deals. They are the absolute easiest and best way to get huge deals on cruises.

For example, I'm on the **American Discount Cruise** website right now looking at a five-night Pacific coastal cruise for $149. That's incredibly cheap.

Here are a list of preferred cruise agencies that offer last-minute cruises. Once you find a good deal, I recommend calling them to try to push the price even lower. If they don't think they'll sell the ticket otherwise, you can get an even better deal.

American Discount Cruise:
www.americandiscountcruises.com/sales/last-minute-cruises.html
Avoya Travel: www.avoyatravel.com
CruCon Cruise Outlet: www.crucon.com

If You Don't Book With a Travel Agent, Do This

The only problem with using an agent is they often tack up the price to juice their commissions. Yes, you'll get better deals than most, but you want the unpublished rates *without* an agent, right?

Here's how you get around that and make everyone happy.

Before you go straight to your travel agent, do this first. Go to an agent of the cruise line you plan to take and book your cruise for a better deal. Tell them exactly what you want — and what price you want it for.

Then, if you get the better deal, transfer the booking to your travel agent. That way, your travel agent still gets the volume credit.

Depending on how appreciative your agent is of this gesture, you could find your room stocked with bottles of wine, fruit baskets, etc.

Perks of Being a Socialite

Attend any and all events that interest you on the cruise. Not only will you meet interesting (and possibly influential) people, you're likely to get free drinks.

For example, if there's an art auction going on in the cruise you're sailing on, go. Art auctions and/or showings normally have free drinks and food.

Get on the Captain's VIP List

Everyone on a cruise wants to eat with the captain. But not

everyone knows how to get on his VIP list.

Here's how...

Normally, the captain invites only individuals who have received a referral. These referrals are normally passed down from the corporate office. How do you get a referral? Simple. You can write corporate yourself or get someone to write corporate for you.

If your company has worked with the cruise line in the past, use that. Get your boss to write the cruise line.

If, for whatever reason, this isn't possible, you can still send a request yourself. Give them a good reason why they should pick YOU (preferably one that benefits them), and you'll dramatically raise your chances of getting picked.

Get Paid to Cruise

Many cruise ships are looking for men and women to entertain the guests. If you're a social butterfly, this job is perfect for you. And it comes with plenty of attractive perks.

The first perk is this: **Your only responsibility is to have fun with the guests**. The other perk is that social hosts normally have an open tab and eat for free on most nights.

Average compensation: $1,500–2,000 a month plus free room, board and drinks

Here are three more of the most common jobs available.

Art Auctioneer

It's common for a cruise ship to have a gallery or two on board. The art auctioneer is responsible for selling and bidding the pieces to passengers.

Average compensation: $2,000–4,000 a month plus free room

Assistant Cruise Director

The assistant cruise director (ACD) is one of the most demanding jobs — but it could also be the most rewarding for the right person. As an ACD, you'll be required to attend social events, dinners, and evening shows and make regular social appearances. You'll help the passengers on and off the ship, and you'll be their go-to person for anything they may need.

Average compensation: $1,500–1,500 a month plus free room and board.

Instructor/Speaker

Whether you teach yoga, dance, or diving or do speaking engagements... a cruise ship is a perfect way to get paid to do what you love. It's common for cruises to offer instructors from all types of different backgrounds and skills.

Average compensation: $1,750–2,000 plus free room and board.

More Info

Use these links to learn more about how you too can cruise for free:

Cruise Ship Jobs Network:
www.cruiseshipjobsnetwork.com/cruise-staff-jobs.html
CruiseJobFinder:
www.cruisejobfinder.com/JobDescriptions/activity_
entertainment_jobs.php
JobMonkey:
www.jobmonkey.com/cruise/html/hosts_and_hostesses.html
Compass Speakers:
www.compassspeakers.com/gentleman_host.html

Get Free Drinks on Your Next Flight

The biggest secret to getting free drinks on your next flight is to steer clear of U.S. airlines. They're sticklers for overpricing those alcoholic drinks. With the tentative exceptions of American Airlines and Delta, you'd be hard-pressed to find a free drink floating in a U.S. airline.

Fortunately, though, **Map Happy** has created a comprehensive list of airlines that serve free alcohol. Enjoy.

The Ultimate List of Free Flight Drinks:

www.maphappy.org/2012/07/wine-the-ultimate-list-of-airlines-that-serve-free-alcohol

Free Museum Visits

If you have a **Bank of America** or **Merrill Lynch** debit or credit card, you're eligible for free tickets to museums and around 150 other cultural places on the first weekend of every month.

If you don't have either, I can recommend one card.

The **Travel Rewards card from Bank of America**. This card not only allows you to access 150 museums across the country for free, but also gives you 10,000 bonus points to use toward your next trip. You can use these points for airfares or hotels. To receive them, though, you must charge at least $500 on the card in the first 90 days. You could easily accomplish this by just using it for normal expenses. And there's no annual fee.

www.bankofamerica.com/credit-cards/overview.go

Members-Only Complimentary Tickets

Here's a great tip for free (and deeply discounted) tickets for theater, comedy, sports, music, performing arts... and even special events like wine tastings, sushi making classes, and rodeos.

The company is called **Gold Star**. They work with more than 4,000 venues and entertainment producers across the country and offer the world's largest selection of discounted tickets. Sign up at goldstar.com and join 4 million members who receive members-only complimentary tickets.

Goldstar: www.goldstar.com

Free Campgrounds

The cheapest and simplest way to travel as an American is to get in touch with the homeland and camp across the States. Finding free camping grounds is extremely easy.

A number of states in the U.S. provide you with free camp-grounds in their national parks, city parks, county parks, and national forests.

Visit freecampsites.net and then click on the state where you are planning to go for a camping trip.

Free Camp Sites: **www.freecampsites.net**

Free Passport Photos

ePassportPhoto believes there's no reason you should have to spend valuable time and money just to get a compliant set of passport photos.

Unlike most photo shops, their system will provide you with precise government requirements of over 60 countries of your choosing.

They give you three options: You can choose a drugstore pickup for as little as $1.50 per photo. You can choose to have them mail your photo to you home for as little as $1.50. Or you can choose their Do-It-Yourself service for FREE.

ePassportPhoto: **www.epassportphoto.com**

Free Road Maps

While travelling, get free road maps by visiting heyitsfree.net. They offer road maps of almost all the 50 states of U.S., including Alaska, Kansas, and Iowa.

Hey Its Free: **www.heyitsfree.net/free-state-maps**

Deduct Your Next Vacation

There are several ways you can turn your family vacation into a partial tax deduction if the travel expenses are necessary for your job or business.

[BONUS TIP: Travel expenses are deductible if you're looking for a job, even if you don't get it. For more valuable tax tips, see Chapter Sixteen.]

To deduct the cost of your vacation, the trip must be within the U.S. and primarily (over 50%) for business. If going abroad, the trip must be over 75% business to deduct the cost of more than one week of travel.

The beauty of this trick is that bringing your family along for a business trip won't disqualify you from writing off anything that you wouldn't normally be able to deduct. There is a limit, of course. You can't write off all of your family's expenses. Only expenses you would normally make are deductible. But this can still work in your favor.

For example, you can write off a rental car because it would cost the same either way. You can't, on the other hand, write off individual airfare tickets aside from your own.

Here's all of what's deductible:

- Airplane, train, bus, or car, between your home and destination and while at your destination

- Meals (50% deductible) and lodging
- Fares for taxis and other forms of transportation
- Other business expenses like seminar and conference fees, dry cleaning and laundry, business calls, computer and Internet fees, etc.

For more information on how to deduct your vacation, visit the link below.

Deduct your vacation:

www.seldenfox.com/how-to-make-your-vacation-a-tax-deduction

Chapter Two:
Life's Luxuries

Free Gold, Silver, Art and Antiques

You're about to take advantage of one of the United States' greatest mass movements. And if you do it right, you'll get free gold, silver, art, antiques, jewelry, and much more.

Some are calling it The Economy 2.0. It's a way to get rid of what you don't want and collect what you do in return. There are a few little-known sites that allow you to give up your old stuff for credits and then use those credits to get the stuff you want.

But if you act quick on what you're about to learn, you'll be able to collect gold, silver, art, and antiques, **without giving up a thing**.

Here's how...

Listia is an auction site that offers all sorts of items — from jewelry and precious metals to electronics and art — for no cost at all (except sometimes the cost of shipping).

For a limited time, you can receive more than 4,000 credits for free just for signing up and watching their tutorial videos. These credits allow you to bid on gold, silver, collectible coins, art, antiques, and much more.

For example, I used 499 credits to bid on a free silver bar and won. I used another 499 credits and won a foreign coin, a bank note, a wheat penny, a jade silver ring, and two trading cards.

I had to pay a small shipping fee for these, but oftentimes you can get items shipped to your house for free.

To get the *really good stuff*, you may have to sell stuff you no longer want to get more credits. But if you're due for a good cleaning, it could be a win-win.

Sign up at the link below to get started!

Listia: **www.listia.com**

Also, take a look at **Yerdle**. Although it's newer and less established, you might find some useful stuff for free.

Yerdle: **www.yerdle.com**

Free Land and Homes

The Homestead Act is back.

Different towns, like Beatrice, Nebraska, are offering free land. There are two stipulations: You need to be at least 21 years of age and live on that land for an agreed-upon amount of time. Some of the agreements maintain that you must build a home, some of them have a home on them, and some are fine if you simply park an RV there.

Of course, homesteading incentives are nothing new. They date back to 1862, when the original Homestead Act helped settle harder-to-reach areas of the States.

Here are a few resources you'll find useful if you're interested in claiming some free land for yourself.

Quick intro to homesteading:
www.eartheasy.com/blog/2011/10/free-land-are-you-ready-to-try-homesteading
All states participating:
www.cfra.org/renewrural/freeland#more

Get A Free Car

There are many places that claim to give you a free car wrapped in advertisements. Unfortunately, my team and I couldn't find one website that actually delivered on this promise.

We're sure they exist and encourage you to do your own research if this is something that interests you. But since we couldn't verify it, this secret didn't to make it in your copy of *Laissez Faire's Big Book of Free*.

But there are plenty of legit offers you can use to **get a new car and have it pay for itself each month**.

Some of them require work, but as you'll soon see, it's probably work you're already doing. Other tricks will require a minimal amount of work that I'm sure you won't mind doing in exchange (if you really do want that new car, that is).

Ordinary folks all over America are doing exactly what you're about to learn all about. They are getting brand-new cars, paid in full each month.

We'll start with just one way we've uncovered:

Make $55/Hour Without Leaving Your Neighborhood

With car sharing services like **Uber** and **Lyft**, *anyone* can quickly and easily turn their cars into taxi cabs for their communities.

Many people are catching onto this simple way to make good money on the side. These services have gained massive popularity over the past couple years.

One driver, in a recent interview with Business Insider, revealed how much he made as an Uber driver: "The max I've made on an hourly basis is about $5–55 an hour. The average on it is about $27 per hour."

For more information on how it works, and how you can get started in your free time, here are the only links you'll need to get you started.

UBER: www.Uber.com

LYFT: www.Lyft.com

Help Your Community (And Get Paid)

There are several sites you can use to do small tasks for people in your community. Anyone can outsource their chores, errands, and tasks to anyone else who is willing to do them. **TaskRabbit** is one of the more well-known sites, but far from the only one.

TaskRabbit: **www.taskrabbit.com**

[NOTE: For a full list of free ways to make money, check out Chapter Twelve.]

Make Money While You Run Errands

Every time you go to the grocery store only for yourself, you're missing out on a great income opportunity. Most people these days are so busy they'd LOVE another set of hands helping them with their errands.

Offer to pick up groceries for your neighbors for a small fee. All you'll be able to handle is one or two more people, and that's all you'll need. Charge them 15% of their bill. So if you spend $100 on their groceries a week, that's $60 a month per person, $120 for two families.

Deliver Organic Vegetables to Restaurants

If you want to get creative, take a lesson from the Brazilians. In Brazil, you see many small entrepreneurs delivering produce to restaurants from nearby farms.

Restaurant owners, no matter where they are, always look for ways to streamline their business. And many will pay top dollar if you're reliable and can help them do that. Likewise, small farmers are looking for outlets for their crops. Many of them are forced to give much of their produce away because they can't sell it in time.

That's where you come in. If you know of any organic growers in your area, approach them and create a list of what they have and what they project they'll have in the coming weeks and months. Approach restaurant owners with this list and see if they are interested.

Cut a deal with the restaurant owners and promise a cut to the farmers... and you're in business. Start small and slow and you'll be making money in no time.

Take the Dogs to the Groomers

Have a dog? You have to go to the groomer anyway, why not take a couple more? Go beyond your circle of friends and neighbors and post an ad on Craigslist or **TaskRabbit**.

Craigslist: www.craigslist.com

TaskRabbit: www.taskrabbit.com

Take Neighborhood Kids to School

Same idea as above. If you're taking your kids to school, why not carpool and charge a nominal fee for your time and gas?

Go on Airport/Appointment Runs for Your Community

Next time you're talking with your neighbors, just throw this idea out there. Especially if they go out of town a lot. Remember, many families are so busy, they'd would love it if you gave them a helping hand for a small fee. So help them!

Free Car:
The One-Day-a-Month Workweek

OK. What if you don't want to — or don't have the time to — drive around all day? The opportunities I showed you are great. But they're not for everyone.

Here's an even simpler way to get that brand-new car paid for. The best part about this little-known hack is you do very little work — and could *easily* earn your monthly car payment in less than a week. Maybe even a day.

Services like **RelayRides** and **Getaround** make it easy for you to rent out your car for hours, days, or weeks at a time. You arc in control of how long a renter can have your car, long before their feet touch the pedals.

You can create a new listing in minutes. All you need is a couple pictures of your car.

How much money could I make? Depending on the make and model, you could make up to $1,500 per week or $300 per day. Meaning, one week (or one day) could easily pay your entire month's payment.

And what if a renter gets into an accident? You're covered by $1 million liability insurance policy that protects you during every rental. It covers damage to or theft from your car. As an extra measure of coverage, these services screen each renter and deny access to those with a bad driving history or un-confirmed identity. Also, you decide who gets to rent your car and when.

RelayRides: www.relayrides.com

Getaround: www.getaround.com

Get Paid to Drive

There are two ways you can get paid to test-drive new cars.

One, **local dealer incentives**.

Car dealerships offer incentives to customers who are willing to test out their new cars. That's right. You'll receive cash or gift cards just for driving other people's cars.

Two, you can **evaluate dealerships**.

With this gig, you go in as an undercover shopper who pretends to be in the market for a new car. Your job is to evaluate things like customer service and quality of sales presentation. Normally, you'll be required to take a test-drive.

Afterward, you'll write a short report on the dealership you visited. Most companies will pay you $50 per dealership.

Here are some of the best undercover shopping companies in the United States:

BestMark ($20–30 per gig):
www.bestmark.com/become_a_shopper.htm
Sinclair Service Assessments ($60 per gig):
www.sinclaircustomermetrics.com
Business Evaluation Services ($50 per gig):
www.intelli-shop.com

Free Car Rental Insurance

Many people don't know this, but many credit card companies offer free insurance when you use their card to pay for a rental car. Before I show you how the benefits offered by each company, here's what you need to know first:

Your credit card offers secondary insurance. Meaning, it will pay the cost of certain damages your regular insurance won't.

You must book the rental car with your credit card under your name in order to receive coverage. And in most cases, you must refuse coverage offered by the rental car agency.

Also, make sure you do your homework before trying this. Some credit card issuers don't offer car rental insurance at all. That's why it's a great idea to call your bank and ask about your specific card's benefits.

Here's the quick-and-dirty breakdown:

VISA: Unlike other companies, Visa offers rental car insurance on all their cards — Standard, Signature, rewards, all of them. But one caveat is that they limit their rental period to 15 days. Visa puts emphasis on the fact that these terms vary bank-to bank.

MASTERCARD: Rental insurance is offered only on Platinum, Gold, World, and World Elite cards. Coverage lasts up to 31 consecutive days.

AMERICAN EXPRESS: AmEx offers free secondary coverage up to $50,000 ($75,000 on the American Express Platinum and Delta Reserve cards), and offers premium coverage for a fee. The free coverage lasts up to 30 days, the premium, 42 days.

DISCOVER: Discover cards are the worst for rental insurance. The coverage is limited to only a few cards (the **Motiva**, **Miles**, and **Open Road**), and these cards cover far less than other networks.

For more detailed information on what each network covers, visit this link:

www.nerdwallet.com/blog/credit-card-benefits/rental-car-insurance

Make Big Oil Pay Your Gas Bill

What you're about to learn is known, by the few who take advantage of it, as the "**10-86 Gas Pump Payback Plan**."

It's an ingenious way to make Big Oil pay your gas bill each and every month. And here's the kicker...

The IRS can't touch a penny of those profits.

Sounds amazing, right?

Neil George is Agora Financial's income expert and editor of *Lifetime Income Report*. He's also well versed in these 10-86 Payback Plans. We've invited him to explain how you can get into these plans as soon as today — and start receiving paybacks from Big Oil.

Oil companies primarily stick to extracting oil and gas from the ground. Some refine it. Some even store it. But that's where their job ends. They leave it to others to figure out how to get it where it needs to go.

One of the safest, fastest, and most reliable ways to move oil is through pipelines. But building them is a real pain. You have to deal with geographic challenges, and of course the legal challenges — from the individual districts you want to build through all the way up to the navigating the Environmental Protection Agency. Then after all that, you still need to build the thing!

Frankly, the initial costs outweighed future benefits, so Big Oil didn't want to take the risks involved.

That's where Reagan's 10-86s come in. The Reagan administration knew this infrastructure was important, but wanted to leave it in the hands of private businesses. So they convinced Congress to add a loophole to tax laws, effectively creating master limited partnerships.

Reagan signed the law in October 1986 — which is why we call them 10-86 companies.

Here's how it works: In exchange for putting up tons of money upfront to build the pipelines, 10-86 companies get lucrative tax breaks down the road.

It's a great deal for them, because once a pipeline is built, there are few ongoing costs. Instead, they receive a lot of income — the money Big Oil companies pay the pipelines to ship their products.

And thanks to the tax incentives, the 10-86s pay zero corporate taxes on that income. That's right — all that incoming cash cannot be touched by the IRS.

The catch is that 10-86s must pay out a large portion of that income to unit holders (basically the same as shareholders). Not surprisingly, a majority of the unit holders are the Big Oil companies themselves. But they are also available to investors through the regular stock markets, where they trade just like stocks, too.

Not only can they pay large distributions, they are forced to do so. At least 90% of their profits must go back to shareholders.

Because of this extraordinarily high payout ratio, 10-86s sport extra-high yields.

And right now, there's never been a better time to buy into these special investments. Remember, the more profits a 10-86 receives, the more it must pay out by law. So thanks to a shift in the oil business, pipeline companies are poised to see bigger profits in the months ahead!

Neil recommended his Lifetime Income Report readers buy into **Sunoco Logistics Partners (NYSE: SXL)** to get a piece of this action.

According to Neil, it's fast growing; it offers a high, well-covered dividend; and its unit price is stable in both up and down markets. It currently pays a 3.6% yield.

Action to take: Units of Sunoco Logistics Partners (NYSE: SXL) are currently a buy up to $66.76.

Buy enough so the dividends cover your gas bill each month and make Big Oil pay you back!

[NOTE: Neil recommends two more 10-86 companies to his **Lifetime Income Report** *readers. One is currently yielding over 4% and has made some readers up to 215% gains. Another pays above a whopping 6%. To learn more, check out his letter at www.agorafinancial.com.]*

Free Money: Make $1,425 This Year With These 5 Alliances

If you don't want to use your credit card rewards points for travel or hotels, you can always redeem them for cold hard cash.

As a general rule, for every 10,000 points you earn, you'll get $100. There are five credit card promotions currently running (at the time of writing) that could bring you $1,425 this year. That's free money.

For all the details, head over to The Penny Hoarder blog.

Five credit card promotions that will make you $1,425:

www.thepennyhoarder.com/5-credit-card-promotions-that-made-me-1375

Two Free Passive Income Opportunities

This is about as simple as it gets.

Google and a company called Media Insiders Panel want to pay you to install two apps on your smartphone. You don't have to do anything but keep them installed and you'll receive a check each month.

First, let me tell you about **Media Insiders Panel**.

This company helps media companies better understand how you consume and share media.

According to their website, the app "measures activities conducted on a device, such as sharing, viewing, clicking, chatting, downloading, and more. The app also listens for TV shows" and identifies what TV shows were watched.

I know what you're thinking... it sounds weird to let them track you at all times. If privacy is a major concern, this app isn't for you.

But if you're interested, they do have a strict privacy protection policy and vow to never share or release your personal information. So it all comes down to your comfort level with them tracking your data usage.

How much will I make? The **Media Insiders** app could make you up to $185 per year, without you lifting a finger.

You can get more information about this application and install it at this website:

www.mediainsiderspanel.com/Portal/default.aspx

Google Screenwise is your second moneymaking opportunity.

This app runs similar to Media Insiders', only it operates on the Google Chrome browser. The panel who will receive this data help Google better understand how what time of day people browse most, how long they stay on specific websites, and what sites are most popular.

How much money will I make? Google gives out $8 after seven days of signing up and $2 every week. Meaning, you could make up to $112 per year in passive income on **Google Screenwise**.

Sign up here: www.screenwisetrends.com

Added up, you could make **$295 per year** with both of these applications. (For more tips just like this one, check out:

www.thepennyhoarder.com)

I know what you're thinking... $295 a year isn't worth your time, right? Wrong. Because next I'm going to show you how to turn that $295 into $132,000.

How To Turn $295 into $132,000

It's called "**peer-to-peer lending**." And it could change the way you invest forever.

Peer-to-peer lending lets you, the investor, loan average Americans money when they can't get it from the bank — or when the bank terms are too harsh. Potential borrowers are screened and scored for creditworthiness. You review their accounts and what they plan to use the money for and negotiate an interest rate, which you can set higher than 14%. In fact, 14% is the average interest rate on peer-to-peer lending website **Lending Club**.

After you agree on an interest rate, borrowers will make fixed monthly payments directly into your account.

There are several websites that allow you simple, quick access to these deals. I'll give you a list of our top-rated websites in a moment.

For now, let's imagine you invest just the $295 you made from the apps mentioned above. Let's also say you earn, on average, 14% on your money.

If you could just leave that $295 alone for 30 years, it would turn into a whopping $132,000.

Here are the best peer-to-peer websites you'll find online at the time of writing:

LendingClub: www.lendingclub.com

Prosper: www.prosper.com

Lend Academy: www.lendacademy.com

Get Designer Brands
for 60% Off More

If you like designer wear but hate how expensive it is, you need **Gilt**.

Gilt provides instant insider access to some of the world's top designer labels for up to 60% off retail. Also, for each friend that you refer, you'll receive $25 to use toward your next purchase.

Gilt: www.gilt.com

FLIP DESIGNER CLOTHES

Tradesy, **Twice**, and **Threadflip** are three sites that allow anyone to buy and sell their designer wear with other like-minded fashionistas. Check out their sites at:

Tradesy: www.tradesy.com

Twice: www.liketwice.com

ThreadFlip: www.threadflip.com

Never Pay Retail Again

DHgate has revolutionized global trade. Normally, when you buy something overseas, you're forced to buy it in bulk to receive wholesale prices.

Not anymore. **DHgate** has made it possible for you to buy as little as one item (or many more if you're a business owner) at wholesale prices.

DHgate: **www.dhgate.com**

Free Birthday Presents

Add more fun to a birthday party with this little-known website.

Inside, you'll find free gift vouchers, rock climbing sessions, meals, ice cream, car washes, movie rentals, and bowling sessions. Visit freebirthdaytreats.com and talk to the Birthday Freebie Expert who can help you get your free birthday present and aid you in saving $10–100.

Free Birthday Treats: www.freebirthdaytreats.com

Free Bottle Of Wine

The Reverse Wine Snob blog has teamed up with **Clubw** so that you can receive a free bottle of wine.

All you have to do is sign up for **Clubw**, a premier wine curating service, and type in the code "rws" at checkout.

For more information, visit the blog at the following link:

Claim your free bottle of wine:

www.reversewinesnob.com/2012/11/free-bottle-of-wine-and-free-shipping-from-club-w.html

Chapter Three:
Essential Services

Power Your Home For Free

What if you could eliminate the need for a power bill? Imagine your power company paying YOU for the energy your house is creating. The most obvious option is to build your own solar panels. If you're looking for a good return on your investment, it's hard to beat solar.

If you take advantage of all the rebates and tax incentives that exist, not to mention how much your home's value will increase, your do-it-yourself solar costs can be recouped in just a few years. After that, you'll enjoy decades of guilt- and cost-free power for your home.

Best part? You can learn every bit of how to do it for FREE. **SolPowerPeople** offers free live monthly lectures by some of the world's top solar experts. These experts provide great training that you can follow at your own pace.

Free solar panel course:

www.solpowerpeople.com/solarmooc-academy

Make Your Home Safer With A Free Gun Lock

If you have a gun and are worried that your kids might mess with it, then why not get a free gun lock? All you have to do is visit projectchildsafe.org to claim yours today.

Project ChildSafe: **www.projectchildsafe.org**

Free RVs and Cars
For Your Next Vacation

These three words will get you a free RV or car (plus a little gas money): **vehicle relocation services**.

Every single day, companies across the U.S. are looking for people to move cars, SUVs, and even RVs to where they need them. This is great news for you.

Why? Because you can take that cross-country trip... go visit the family... or just check out a city you've been dying to see... and get there absolutely free.

The most well-known service for vehicle relocation services is called **Auto Driveaway**. Visit this link for a list of cars on their website you could drive away in as soon as next week:

www.autodriveaway.com/view_car_list

And here's one company you can contact to get started:

Professional Automotive Relocation Services Inc. (PARS):

www.parsinc.com

RV Relocation Services

Rent an RV for as little as $1 a day — sometimes FREE. Also, many offers include up to a $300 gas stipend.

Apollo RV: www.apollorv.com/reloc.aspx

Imoova: www.imoova.com/imoova/relocations

Free Shipping, Everywhere

Never pay shipping again. One website allows you to get free shipping from over 1,500 stores worldwide. There are no minimums to spend, you can still use rebates and coupons to shop, and you receive FREE return shipping too.

Free shipping: **www.freeshipping.com/Join**

Free Car Maintenance

Stop paying for your car maintenance every time it experiences an issue. Many companies offer some form of free car maintenance. The trick is knowing which company offers what and going to that one to get your car fixed.

For Tire Repair and Rotation

Pep Boys will repair and rotate your tires for free, even if you didn't buy your tires from them.

To see if there's a Pep Boys near you, visit this website:
storelocator.pepboys.com/pepboys

Windshield Wiper Installation

AutoZone, **O'Reilly**, and **Advance Auto Parts** will replace your wiper blades for free. The only caveat is, you must have bought the originals at the store you're requesting the blades from.

Also, if you have a **Sam's Club** membership, this service is always free, no matter where you got the blades.

To see if there's an AutoZone in your area, visit this link:
www.autozone.com/autozone/storelocator/
storeLocatorMain.jsp

For the O'Reilly store locator:

www.oreillyauto.com/site/fi/storelocator.oap

And for Advance Auto Parts stores:

shop.advanceautoparts.com/web/StoreLocatorView

Battery Test and Charge

Pep Boys, **AutoZone**, **Firestone**, and **Advance Auto Parts** will all test your battery for free. They'll be able to tell you in minutes whether you need a new one, or if it just needs charged. **AutoZone** has a Fast Charger that they'll charge your battery with if that's the case. And yes, that's free too.

Find a Firestone store near you here:

www.firestonecompleteautocare.com/locate

Diagnostic Test

Pep Boys will check your brakes and your brake fluid for free. They'll also check your alignment while they're at it.

Meineke and **AAMCO** also offer free brake tests.

Free Cab Ride

What's The Catch?

The catch is they want you in the door. Free stuff will do that. Eventually, if they treat you well enough, they know you'll purchase their brakes, tires, and services.

Join **Lyft** and **Uber** and your first ride is on them. They are both services that allow anyone in your community to become a taxi driver. Sign up today and get a $25 credit toward your first ride.

Lyft: www.lyft.com
Uber: www.uber.com

Free Lifesaving Device

If you or a family member is susceptible to potentially life-threatening allergic reactions (anaphylaxis), the website you'll learn about in a moment could change your life.

Life-threatening reactions to things like bee stings, peanuts, or seafood can happen anywhere at any time. And an EpiPen could be the one thing to save your life.

An EpiPen is a self-injectable device (auto-injector) that contains epinephrine — the first-line treatment for severe allergic reactions. They are so easy to use that some of them "talk" you through exactly how to use them. And today you're going to learn a little-known loophole for receiving these pens for free.

Use the links below to learn how to receive these pens absolutely free.

For more information, and to learn how you can claim your free EpiPens, visit the **My Life and Kids** blog.

FREE EpiPens:

www.mylifeandkids.com/how-to-get-free-epipens/

FREE TALKING EpiPens:

www.mylifeandkids.com/the-talking-epipen-and-how-to-get-it-for-free-auvi-q

Fight Insurance Snobs And Save A Bundle

Most Americans simply renew their coverage every year instead of shopping around. If there's one thing to learn in this book, it's this: Don't be like most Americans. Your insurance salesman will never tell you, but you're probably spending too much on insurance. In fact, you could be overpaying by as much as 50%.

But now you don't have to. There are plenty of free insurance shopping websites that will show you the absolute best deals you're eligible for. With the three I'm about to show you, you could save hundreds of dollars this year in just a few minutes.

Insure: www.insure.com

InsWeb: www.insweb.com

NetQuote: www.netquote.com

For more ways to save on normal expenses, visit this link: www.bottomlinepublications.com/content/article/wealth-a-retirement/how-to-save-5-000-a-year-on-expenses-everyone-has

Chapter Four:
Books

Free Books On Amazon

First things first. Here's the simplest way to get free books:

Get an Amazon rewards card.

You may've noticed that credit cards come up a lot in this book. It's for a good reason. If your credit is sound, credit card companies are constantly duking it out for your business. That means there are ALWAYS attractive offers to sink your teeth into. Offers that will bring you what is essentially FREE money.

For example, Amazon has introduced a **Rewards Visa Card** that lets you swap credit card points for free items, including books. For every dollar you spend, you receive a point. You get three points if you use your card at a restaurant or gas station.

With every 100 points you collect, $1 will be added to your account. At the time of writing, Amazon is offering to add a free gift card worth $30 just for signing up, so keep your eye out for those deals, too.

Amazon Rewards:

www.amazon.com/rewards

Free Audiobooks

LibriVox is a noncommercial, nonprofit, and ad-free project that creates FREE audiobooks. They are powered by volunteers and want to make all of their books in the public domain available for free, in audiobook form.

To see their full collection, visit the link below.

LibriVox: **www.librivox.com**

And here are 550 more audiobooks from **Open Culture**.

Open Culture audiobooks:

www.openculture.com/freeaudiobooks

Build Your Own (Digital) Library For Free

Here's how you can get over 45,000 books mailed to your doorstep for free. Sound crazy? Hear me out.

Project Gutenberg is the first and largest single collection of electronic books (or e-books) on the Internet. With the help of thousands of volunteers, this organization digitized a good chunk of the greatest books in history.

Right now, they are offering to send anyone who wants one a CD filled with 29,500 books — FREE.

To request yours, visit the link below.

FREE Gutenberg CD:

www.gutenberg.org/wiki/Gutenberg:The_CD_and_ DVD_Project

Bonus tip: All books in the Gutenberg file are in the public domain. Current copyright laws state that 70 years after an author's death, his or her books fall into the public domain. If you prefer to have a hard copy of ANY of the 45,000 books in their collection, you're legally allowed to do so. So here's how you can get ANY book you want for cost.

CreateSpace is a print-on-demand (POD) self-publishing platform. Print-on-demand means that when you use their service, they'll print your book when you buy it online and send it to you.

This makes sure you never have any overhead when publishing your book. What's more, you can publish your book (and get it listed on Amazon.com) for free on their platform.

More on that later.

To get your Gutenberg books in print, all you have to do is...

1. Set up a free CreateSpace account.
2. Upload the file you received from Gutenberg.
3. And print the book!

All you'll pay is the cost to print the book.

More Free Books

Gutenberg is far from the only company offering free e-books. Check out the links below for even more.

BookZZ: www.bookzz.org

Open Culture: www.openculture.com/free_ebooks

Free-Ebooks.net: www.free-ebooks.net

Open Library: www.openlibrary.org

Internet Archive: www.archive.org/details/texts

ManyBooks.net: www.manybooks.net

Book Swap

Can't find the book you want for free? Don't buy it just yet.

Try out a company called **PaperBack Swap**. It's exactly as it sounds. You swap books your books with other users. They have a database of over 4 million books to choose from. All you pay for is the shipping.

PaperBack Swap: www.paperbackswap.com

Free And Almost-Free Textbooks

It's ridiculous what they charge these days for school textbooks.

Each book can cost $200 or much more. The kicker is that this book will be nearly worthless soon after you buy it, when a new edition comes out. Here are a few ways you can "hack" your college textbooks.

Make A Copy

This technique works best on small textbooks.

Simply buy the book, photocopy and bind it together, and then return the book for a full refund. Though it'll take some time, it could mean the difference between paying $15 and $350.

Book too big?

Try A Rental

FreeTextbooks is a company that allows you to rent your books from other students for a MUCH lower price than buying them. Here's how it works:

1. **Rent:** Find the books you need and select how long you need them for. Add them to your cart and check out.
2. **Get:** Feel free to highlight, but they don't allow renters to write in the books. Just use your book as

you would normally.

3. **Return:** Ship the book back and you're done!

FreeTextbooks: **www.freetextbooks.com**
If that fails, try this...

Try to Find it For Free

You might be able to find the book you're looking for online on one of these free textbook websites.

Bookboon: **www.bookboon.com**
Boundless: **www.boundless.com**
Open Culture:
www.openculture.com/free_textbooks

Free Advance and/or Autographed Books

How do regular folks get their hands on books signed by their favorite authors? Well, most of the time you have to go to a reading by the author and wait in line. But what if you could receive one from the comfort of your own home? And for free?

Goodreads wants to make that happen for you. Publishers are always giving out free books. All you have to do in return is tell them what you think. And Goodreads has become the perfect middleman.

Just go to **www.goodreads.com/giveaway** and enter for advanced copies of pre-release books.

You get to choose which books you want to enter for and again. And once you win one, you'll receive it totally free, including the postage. If you're lucky, you may even get freebies like bookmarks, autographs, or lights with every book you receive.

Goodreads: **www.goodreads.com/giveaway**

Get New Releases For Free

You just learned how to get pre-released books for free. Now here's how you get new releases on **Amazon**.

We all know new releases cost a lot more than books that have been around for a while — but who has the patience to wait for one to become affordable? By then, it's old news.

Amazon has made it easier than ever with one little-known elite community.

Have you ever heard of **Amazon Vine**? I didn't until my research team stumbled upon this hidden club during our research.

It's free to join, but not everyone can get in. Which is why very few people tend to know about it.

Joining Amazon Vine happens only through invitations. Amazon must notice you and invite you to join. There's no other way of getting in.

So how do I get in? It's actually pretty simple. Just write helpful reviews on Amazon.

Each time you write a review on Amazon, readers who read your review can let Amazon know if it was helpful. The more readers who tell Amazon your reviews are helpful, the more Amazon will sit up and pay attention to you.

From their website: "Customers who consistently write helpful reviews and develop a reputation for expertise in specific product categories are most likely to be invited into the program."

Then, you can join the ranks of people like Michael Erb, who was once ranked No. 1 customer reviewer on Amazon. Companies are practically begging him to review their products in exchange for freebies.

Here's what Bill told NPR in an interview:

"I have so many Bluetooth speakers, it's ridiculous. I've got enough lithium-ion batteries in my house to blow up a city block... Literally every other day, there's UPS boxes piled up at the door."

At least once each month, Amazon sends Erb a list of products. He is allowed to choose any two.

"My only obligation," he explained, "is that I need to write a review of those two items within 30 days. And I get to keep the items after I review them."

Through Vine, Michael has received everything from cheap pairs of headphones and high-end laser printers to a $1,000 spin bike. In all, he's received thousands of dollars worth of merchandise.

Here's a simple but effective explanation of how you can become a Vine member:

www.makeuseof.com/tag/amazon-vine-reviewer-free-stuff

Free Bibles For You
And Your Friends

Here's how you get a free Bible. Don't worry, it doesn't involve sneaking one out of a church or someone's home. All you have to do is go online.

Log on to **www.biblesforamerica.org**. By clicking on "Order," you can get one at no cost.

Another option is to log onto www.myfreebible.org. Just click on "Request Your Bible."

Need more? Here are more places you can request a free Bible:

Search God's Word: **www.searchgodsword.com**
Free Bibles: **www.freebibles.net**
FreeBibleSociety.org: **www.freebiblesociety.org**
Get Your Free Bible: **www.getyourfreebible.com**
Cross Walk: **www.crosswalk.com**
Blue Letter Bible: **www.blueletterbible.com**

Chapter Five: Talk. Text. Mail. Free.

Save A Ton On Your Cellphone Bill

If you have a cellphone through a well-known provider, there's a 99.9% chance you're paying WAY too much on your cellphone bill. In fact, you're probably overpaying by more than 50%. Yeah, it's that bad.

The average smartphone user pays around $110. Little do they know they can receive the same service for less than $50. Added up, that's more than $1,400 over a typical two-year contract.

The solution? **Pay-as-you-go plans**. These plans don't require contracts, and they're normally run by lesser-known, lower-cost providers. What most people don't know is these providers buy access to the very same networks that major provider use, so the quality of service should be just as good.

Here are some companies to look into...

Straight Talk: Unlimited talk and text. 2.5 GB of data. $45 per month. No overages. If you go over the 2.5 GB (most smartphone users use 2 GB per month), you'll be throttled down to a slower speed.

www.straighttalk.com

GoSmart Mobile: Unlimited talk and text and 5 GB of data for $45 per month. It operates on the T-Mobile cell network.

www.gosmartmobile.com

Republic Wireless: Unlimited talk, text, and data for $25 per month on 3G network. And its $40 per month on the 4G network. Operates on the Sprint network.

www.republicwireless.com

For more ways to save on common expenses, visit the Bottom Line Publications website at:

www.bottomlinepublications.com/content/article/wealth-a-retirement/how-to-save-5-000-a-year-on-expenses-everyone-has

Free Snail Mail

Even in our ultra-wired world, sometimes you want (or need) to send something via snail mail. Here's how you can get those stamps for free.

Stamps.com: When you open a free trial account on their site, you automatically get $25 to spend toward stamps.

Just make sure you use the stamps and cancel your membership before your trial period is up. Otherwise, they'll automatically charge you a fee each month.

Free Stamps: www.stamps.com

Free Landline Phone Service

Most people have cut the proverbial cord on their landline phones. Why have both a cell phone and a home phone, right?

Well, there are perks of still having a landline. Especially if you can get it for free. Here are some advantages...

No dropped calls. No matter how top-of-the-line your cellphone is, you'll always have the occasional dropped call. That's not the case with landlines.

Emergencies. Let's say you call 911 with an emergency situation. If you call from a cellphone, a dispatcher is going to have trouble pinpointing your exact location. With a landline, they instantly know where you're calling from. Something to consider if you have a family.

Disasters. Think Sept. 11. During that terrifying time cell towers were overloaded with traffic. It was nearly impossible to get a call through. Millions of Americans were left wondering if their loved ones were safe and sound. Though landline phones were likely bogged down a little, you were more likely to receive and call out on one than you were with a cellphone.

So how do I get a free landline?

Ooma provides you with a free landline service.

You will have to pay a one-time fee of $99 for the device and activation. But if you're already paying a landline bill, this upfront cost will pay for itself in no more than a few months.

You'll receive free U.S. calling, caller ID, call waiting, fax mode, and more.

Ooma: **www.ooma.com**

Text For Free

Spend too much to call and text? Try out textPlus.

They'll do everything your phone company does for you at a fraction of the cost — even totally free. There's no signup fee. And no contracts to sign. Just create your free account and they'll give you...

- A free phone number and free unlimited texts to any U.S. or Canadian number
- Free calls to any of the 60 million-plus textPlus users
- The ability to make international calls for pennies on the dollar
- The opportunity to earn FREE minutes with easy and short tasks.

You can use any smartphone or tablet. All you need is a WiFi connection.

Learn more at their website below.

textPlus: **www.textplus.com**

Chapter Six:
World-Class Smarts

Free World-Class Education

Khan Academy is a nonprofit organization with the goal of transforming education forever. They provide world-class education for anyone, anywhere in the world.

The subjects include everything you'd find in a college curriculum. They even have test-prep courses for the SAT, MCAT, and more.

You can track all the courses you've taken, test your knowledge, and set goals for yourself.

Khan Academy: www.khanacademy.com

Another great option is Coursera.

Coursera allows you to take some of the world's best courses for free. They work globally with top universities and organizations to offer online courses that anyone can take, absolutely free.

You can choose from over 400 courses, learn on your own schedule, and test your knowledge with "Mastery Learning" assignments.

Coursera: www.coursera.org

Another great site is edX.

EdX hosts university-level courses from some of the world's best universities. These schools include Stanford, U.C. Berkeley, MIT, Harvard, and the University of Queensland.

Subjects include biology, business, chemistry, computer science, economics, finance, electronics, engineering, food and nutrition, history, humanities, and much more!

edX: **www.edx.org**

The Free Way to Get a Degree

The websites I just showed you are great for learning on your own. Only problem is they won't give you a degree if you finish their courses. But one website we've uncovered will.

University of the People is the world's first nonprofit, tuition-free, accredited academic institution. They're dedicated to opening access to higher education for everyone despite financial, geographical, or societal constraints.

They currently offer four undergraduate degrees: associate and bachelor's degrees in business administration and associate and bachelor's degrees in computer science. These are two fields that are currently in high demand all over the world.

*NOTE: Although **UoPeople is tuition-free, the full ride isn't 100% free**. Students will have to pay an application fee ($10–50) and exam processing fees ($100 per exam).*

If you are unable to afford these fees, they have a variety of scholarship programs (link below.)

For more information, visit the links below.

University of the People: **www.uopeople.edu**

Scholarship Programs:

www.uopeople.edu/groups/dedicated_scholarships

Chapter Seven:
Free Lessons

Learn A New Language For Free

Want to learn a new exotic language without having to pay hundreds of dollars to a language tutor? **Duolingo** has you covered.

Their courses are scientifically proven to help you learn a new language faster and more effectively than university courses. Each course integrates reading, speaking, and listening, so the language soaks in and stays there. Even better, you can learn on your phone while you're on the go.

Duolingo: www.duolingo.com

You can also find more free language courses at:

Open Culture:
www.openculture.com/freelanguagelessons
Live Mocha: www.livemocha.com
Memrise: www.memrise.com
BBC Languages:
www.fsi-language-courses.org/Content.php

Learn To Play An Instrument For Free

PlayPerfect is a free music practice program you can download and start using today. The program "listens" as you play a song and instantly tells you if you played each note right or wrong.

You can learn to play anything from the guitar, piano, violin, cello, bass, flute, clarinet, saxophone, trumpet, to trombone.

Free PlayPerfect software: www.nchsoftware.com/practice

Free Instruments and In-Person Lessons For Kids

Opportunity Music Project is a nonprofit that offers full-tuition scholarships and high-quality instruments for children who can't afford them otherwise.

Scholarship students receive weekly private lessons, are given access to free concerts, and have access to an education series led by professional musicians.

Learn all about this program on their website.

Opportunity Music Project:

www.opportunitymusicproject.org

Learn To Play The Guitar In 10 Hours

If you've ever thought of picking up a guitar but just haven't gotten around to it, the website you're about to see might be all the motivation you'll need.

Set aside 10 hours for practice and you'll be able to play great songs for friends and family — even if you've never played a note.

The 10-hour guitar lesson:

www.tropicalmba.com/learn-to-play-guitar

MORE FREE INSTRUMENT LESSONS

Video tabs (guitar): www.videotabs.com

YouTube (all): www.youtube.com

InstrumentChamp (most): www.instrumentchamp.com

Hoffman Academy (piano): www.hoffmanacademy.com

Free Sheet Music

The **Mutopia Project** offers free sheet music of famous and lesser-known works from Bach, Beethoven, Chopin, Handel, Mozart, and many others.

Mutopia Project: **www.mutopiaproject.com**

Learn How to Sing Like A Star

Anyone can do it, but there's no "magic bullet" to learning how to sing beautifully. It takes work. Especially if you're far from a natural. Luckily, you don't have to pay a penny to learn.

Free Singing Lessons offers an incredibly comprehensive singing course, 100% free. The best part about the course is you can go at your own pace and ask questions about/share your singing results with the rest of the community.

Free Singing Lessons: **www.free-singing-lessons.com**

Learn How to Type Lightning Fast

Do you still use the hunt-and-peck method when you type? Would you like to learn how to type faster?

TypingWeb is devoted to teaching you how to rev up your typing skills 100% free of charge.

No matter what skill level you're at, there's a lesson for you.

TypingWeb: **www.typingweb.com**

Free Yoga

Some yoga classes can cost a lot per class. But that doesn't mean you shouldn't enjoy all the amazing benefits just one session per week of yoga will give you.

Especially when you can learn yoga absolutely free.

DoYogaWithMe has hundreds of high-quality, high-definition, 100% free, streaming yoga classes.

You can search videos by difficulty, length, style, and teacher. DoYogaWithMe: **www.doYogaWithMe.com**

Free Beauty Classes

Sephora, a French brand and chain of cosmetic stores, is currently (and indefinitely) offering free in-store beauty lessons in select stores.

From makeup to skin care, learn what the professional makeup artists know.

See if a store near you is participating at the link below.

Sephora beauty classes:

www.sephora.com/store-locations-events?tab=classes#classes

Chapter Eight:
Free Fun

Free Backstage Passes To Your Favorite Events

Ever wish you could get backstage and mingle with the stars? As you'll learn, it's much easier than you think.

The first step is easy. Decide what show you want to get a backstage pass to. Chances are, you already have one in mind.

Let's say there's a band you've been dying to meet and they're coming to your town in a month. Go fetch one of their CDs and **look at the back for their record label's website address. Plug it into your computer and look for the promotion director and/or the media coordinator's email address**.

Put that aside for now. You're going to need it in a minute.

The second step is also simple. Find a few local papers in your area and fish out the contact lists. Find the editor and/or the photo director's name and contact information. Write these things down.

Then, if you can, visit them at the address provided. Introduce yourself. If you can't talk to them in person, email the editor and/or photo director. Ask if they ever use freelancers.

Freelancer what? Well, that's up to you.

If you have a camera and you've taken a few good shots, tell the appropriate people you're a photographer that's trying to gain proper credentials for events. **Tell them you'll be attending [enter band name]'s concert and will send them pictures free of charge in return for a press pass**.

Same thing goes if you're a pretty good writer. This time, though, you tell them you'll write an article about the event.

You may have to contact/visit a few different papers, but keep trying. One of them is bound to bite. Why wouldn't they? You're offering to do something for free that they normally would pay for.

All you'll need is written verification that you're working for their publication. Ask them for a digital copy, if possible.

Once you receive permission, take the emails you collected earlier from the record label and send them an email with your press credentials attached. They will love you for this. Their job is to track people like you down, so when you come to them, they're delighted to help you out.

It really is as easy as that.

For more detailed information on how this works, visit the webpage below.

BackstageSecret.com:

www.backstagesecret.com/backstage_band_pass.htm

Free Movie Tickets And Screenings

Once you become a member of **gofobo**, you'll get on their list to attend private screenings of some of Hollywood's biggest blockbusters — before anyone else gets to see them.

Membership is 100% free, and it's easy to sign up.

gofobo: **www.gofobo.com**

Same for **Get Screening**, another free screening website. The only big difference is Get Screening seems to have more movie options and notifies you when a new screening is scheduled for your area (you have to set up this feature after you sign up).

Membership is also 100% free.

Get Screening: **www.getscreening.com**

Free Redbox Movies

If you have a Redbox nearby, here's a quick-and-easy way to get free rentals each month.

Each time you rent a DVD from Redbox, you may notice they ask for a promotional code. Using the codes you'll find on **Redbox Codes**' website, you may be able to rent a new movie each week.

Redbox Codes: **www.redboxcodes.com**

The Big List of Free Movies And TV Shows

700 Free Movies Courtest of Open Culture

Watch from a selection of 700 free movies online at **Open Culture**. The selection includes classics, indie films, documentaries, and more.

For the full list, follow the link below.

700 free movies:

www.openculture.com/freemoviesonline

Free Movies and TV Shows

Hulu offers a free ad-supported service that allows you to watch a wide selection of movies and hit TV shows absolutely free.

Hulu: www.hulu.com

Crackle is another great place to go to see full-length Hollywood movies and TV shows for free. With Crackle, unlike other companies like it, there are no subscriptions or commitments involved.

Crackle: www.crackle.com

Wine and Dine For Less Than It Costs To Eat At Home

There are many ways to wine and dine for cheap. But there's only one way I know of that will allow you to eat (and drink) at a restaurant for less than it costs to stay at home.

This technique has two steps.

One, find a restaurant nearby that allows you to bring in your own alcohol (BYOB). Make sure they don't charge a corkage fee.

Meaning you can come in and drink your own alcohol for free.

If this sounds like I'm sending you on a wild goose chase, humor me. I've found over 10 great restaurants right near where I live in Baltimore. To prove that I'm not blowing hot air, most of them are on the list below.

A useful tool you can use is called Yelp. It's a social directory for restaurants in your area, where you and other Yelpers can review restaurants. Just punch in the website address below, and type "BYOB" into the search box.

Yelp: www.yelp.com

Two, head over to one of my favorite discount sites, **Restaurant.com**.

Restaurant.com allows you to buy gift certificates at participating restaurants in your area. Normally, you'll get about 60% off your order. For example, you can purchase a gift certificate worth $25 for only $10... or one worth $100 for only $40.

Not bad, right?

But we're not stopping at just 60%. We want to save even more. And here's how you do it.

Every so often, **Restaurant.com** does a promotion where you can receive gift cards worth $25 for only $4. I'm not talking about once a year, either. I've seen this promotion more than once in the past two months.

Sign up for their updates, and when you see that promotion, *jump on it.* Have your list handy of BYOB (corkage free) restaurants, and find the ones that are participating with Restaurant.com.

Buy as many gift cards as they'll let you. Even if you don't end up using them all, they'll make great (and cheap) gifts. And each time you go out wining and dining, **you'll only spend $8 for every $50 worth of food you eat out. And you'll drink for the same price you would at home**.

Who says eating out has to be expensive?

Restaurant.com: www.restaurant.com

Yelp: www.yelp.com

No corkage fee restaurants in Baltimore:

weblogs.baltimoresun.com/entertainment/dining/reviews/ blog/2008/02/top_ten_byob_restaurants_1.html

Chapter Nine:
Free And Easy
Tech

Build A Free Website
In Minutes

It doesn't matter what kind of website you need, or for what: You can build it fast and free. There are hundreds of options to choose from.

That's why we've narrowed it down to the best three options of 2014, no matter if you're trying to sell a product, show off your work, or start the next big blog.

Here they are:

Wix: Choose from hundreds of designer-made fully customizable templates with Wix. Add a commerce site and blog and connect your work to your social media websites.

www.wix.com

Weebly: Creating a powerful, professional website without any technical skills has never been easier. Weebly's drag-and-drop website builder makes it dead simple to get your site up and running in no time.

www.weebly.com

DoodleKit: Doodlekit is another one-stop shop for building a website in minutes. Choose your template, background, border effects, and fonts and the rest takes care of itself.

www.doodlekit.com

Free Email Reminders

How does it feel when you forget a birthday or when you let slip your own anniversary date? Not good, I know.

Luckily for you, you don't have to worry about that anymore.

Enter **FollowUpThen**.

Sign up for their free service and never miss an important meeting, family member's birthday, or loved one's special day. Setting up a reminder is as easy as sending an email. Learn more at the website link below.

FollowUpThen: **www.followupthen.com**

Test Your IQ For Free

IQ tests are one of the best ways to pinpoint your intellectual strengths and weaknesses. You'll be able to see where you stand with certain skills, thus revealing educational opportunities or unveiling hidden talents.

The IQ test from **Brain Metrix** consists of only 20 questions. It shouldn't take more than 15 minutes to complete, and you'll get your results instantly.

Brain Metrix: www.brainmetrix.com

Free AntiVirus Software

Never pay for antivirus software online. Why? Because you can utilize FREE antivirus software programs that do essentially the same tasks, sometimes better than the paid counterparts.

For that, we recommend **Bitdefender**.

It has all the properties of a great antivirus. It's simple to use and works entirely in the background, and you'll never know it's there unless it is taking care of a problem.

Download it for free at the link below.

Bitdefender:

www.bitdefender.com/solutions/free.html

Free Photo Editing Software

Want to start editing your photos but don't want to shell out hundreds of dollars per year for Photoshop?

You're going to love **Gimp**.

If you're creating a website or blog or just want to share photos on Facebook, you need an image editing program. And aside from being completely free, it does have a few advantages over Photoshop.

One, it's a smaller program, which makes it faster and more stable, especially if you have an older computer.

Two, it's more intuitive and easier to use than Photoshop in many ways.

Three, there are many excellent tutorials on how to use **Gimp**, also free.

Here are a couple links to get you started.

Download Gimp: **www.gimp.org/downloads**
Free Gimp tutorials: **www.gimp.org/tutorials**

Free On-The-Go Internet

Whether you're at the airport or on the beach, **FreedomPop** guarantees high-speed wireless Internet on all your devices — FREE.

Their basic plan costs $0. It gives you up to 500 MB of web-surfing a month. This isn't a lot, but it's enough for light surfing and to check your emails while on the go.

FreedomPop does require you to rent the hardware (you pick from a variety of different devices), which can be as much as $100. But you'll get a refund once you return the equipment.

Upon writing, they're offering a USB device with a 2 GB free data trial run for only $15. Keep your eyes peeled for promotions like this one.

FreedomPop: **www.freedompop.com**

Two Free Alternative To Expensive Computer Software

Computer software can be expensive. If you're in the market, check out these free alternatives first.

Instead of spending cash for Microsoft Word, consider using LibreOffice: www.libreoffice.org

Instead of Microsoft Outlook for your email needs, try Thunderbird: www.mozilla.org/en-GB/thunderbird

Chapter Ten:
Make Sports Free

Get Paid To Play Golf

Does getting paid to play golf sound like a dream come true for you? If so, you're going to love this secret.

Today, you're going to learn how to become a **mystery golfer**.

On top of getting paid to play golf, you'll also receive other perks: the opportunity to get your hands on merchandise, free meals, hotel accommodation, and more.

As a mystery golfer, your job is simple.

You'll be tasked to help country clubs or sports centers to evaluate their customers' satisfaction, staff behavior, and overall progress. Most of your job entails just having fun on the course.

Here's how you do it.

There are a few companies that can put you on the fast track. I'll provide all the links in a moment.

First, to give you an example of what kind of jobs you'll be able to look forward to, I pulled the following from a website forum called **Mystery Shop Forum**. I'll provide the link shortly. The job listing was posted on July 25, 2014.

On the following page is the type of job to look out for.

There must be tons of competition, right? There is. But most golfers know only ONE way of applying to these types of jobs. I'm going to show you a way to beat out the competition.

Golf Mystery Shops, $45.00 shop fee plus reimbursements!!

JenniferS — Posts: 15

* Golf Shop Available * $45.00 Shop Fee *BONUS ADDED*
Dates Available: July and August

Shops available in AL, CT, HI, LA, OH, PA, TX

We fully reimburse you for your green, cart, and range fees plus pay you $45.00. You also get reimbursed $25.00 for your food, drink, and pro-shop purchases. (40.00 of you golf with a friend)
This shop requires you to evaluate the entire course, including playing a full round of golf on the day of the shop. You must have golfed 3 times in the past year. Feel free to bring a friend along.
While you are there, you will evaluate the range, the pro-shop, a beverage cart, and a food location. That way, the whole day is complete!
You must complete a Shop Quiz before you golf if you are new to this project.
There is one online evaluation form to complete when you return from the shop that requires you to upload receipts.

I look forward to working with you!

Jennifer
Jennifer@customerserviceexperts.com

Like This Post

July 25, 2014 01:34PM — #

Many people will simply find the companies that provide these types of jobs and sign up. This is where most people stop. That's why it's important, if you really want to get paid to golf, you keep going.

To get the really good jobs, you're going to have to go one step further. As soon as you've signed up, send their scheduling department a letter. ***Be cordial and keep it short. Tell them these things***:

- Your name
- Your age
- Where you live
- How far you're willing to travel for a gig
- How long you've been golfing
- Why they should pick you.

The last point — *why they should pick you* — is the most

important piece. Really think about why they need you in the first place. They're looking for someone who is sociable, respectable, and knowledgeable about the game who will take the job seriously.

[NOTE: If you really want to go the extra mile, you can always offer to give them something they want first. For example, you can mention golf courses in your area that you think may agree to having a mystery golfer come in and give honest feedback. Give them names and contact numbers. If you know someone in a position of influence at a golf course, better still. Connect them together. They'll repay the favor. Also, you can tell them you are willing to approach these places yourself for them but wanted to check to see what they thought first. Of course, if you say this, you have to follow through. And why wouldn't you? It's a win-win!]

Position yourself as the perfect man for the job without over-selling it. Once you've covered all of these points, or as many as you can, send it out.

Keep going! There's only one more step to seal the deal!

If you haven't heard back after a week or so, give the company's **scheduling department** office a call. I've provided some phone numbers for you below, but if you need any more, you can always find them on the company's **"Contact Us"** link on their website.

Before you call, brush up on what type of person the company is looking for to fill that position. Also become familiar with what their expectations are for a mystery golfer. The more familiar the job seems to you, the more comfortable they will feel giving it to you.

A Quick Note for When You Land Your First Job

Once you get the job, you'll want to keep getting more. So take heed: In most cases, you will need to dress like a golfer: polo-type shirt, slacks or shorts, no jeans. You can bring your clubs and hit balls at the driving range or do some putting, but the key element is blending in. You may bring someone, but your guest must look the part too.

Establish Yourself as a Mystery Golfer

Here's how to establish yourself as a real mystery golfer. First create an account on MysteryShopForum, and introduce yourself. Tell the forum members that you're looking for gigs. Some people might offer valuable insight that I haven't been able to touch in the short amount of space in this section.

Mystery Shop Forum: **www.mysteryshopforum.com**

Apply to These Companies First

Here are the companies you should apply to first.

Mercantile Systems:
www.sassieshop.com/2mercsurveys/index.norm.php
Scheduling Department
Mercantile Systems Inc.
Toll-free phone: 1-888-222-8301
Email: shop@mercsystems.com

MSI Mystery Shopping: www.mysteryshopmsi.com
MSI office hours are 8:30 a.m.–4:30 p.m. Pacific Standard Time, Monday–Friday, observing all major holidays.
Toll-free phone: 1-888-222-8301
Scheduling Department: 888-222-8301, ext. 14 or
shop@mercsystems.com

Bare International Associates:
www.bareinternational.com

Email: BAREcorporate@bareinternational.com

Mr. Guy Caron, vice president and general manager

Ms. Lynne Brighton, senior vice president/sales

Mr. Jason Bare, global business development manager

North America and Corporate Headquarters

3702 Pender Drive, Suite #305

Fairfax, VA 22030

Toll-Free: (800) 296-6699

Local: (703) 591-9870

Fax: (703) 293-3124

Service Scouts:

About page: www.servicescouts.com/about.html

Application page:

www.servicescouts.com/becomescout.html

Contact page: www.servicescouts.com/contact.html

Free Golf Clubs

Warrior Custom Golf Inc. is offering an attractive deal for a limited time. Subscribe to the *Warrior* newsletter and receive a free golf club (S&H is not included).

Free Warrior golf club:

www.warriorcustomgolf.com/subscribe

Free Golf Balls

FreeGolfBalls.com wants to give golfers a chance to try out new golf balls without paying for them. You don't need a credit card, there are no purchases required, *and* you'll receive FREE shipping.

All you have to do is select the type of golf balls you'd like, enter your shipping info, and you're done!

Free golf balls: **www.freegolfballs.com**

Free Wrestling Tickets

Are you in the military or know someone who is? If so, here's some good news if you're into professional wrestling.

WWE is providing all military personnel with free tickets to live events. If you are in the military, simply log onto their website and claim your free tickets.

WWE: www.wwe.com

Chapter Eleven: Business And Finance

Start Your Own Business For Free

OK, so you have a brilliant idea for a new product, but don't have the cash — or connections with the cash — to get started.

Ten years ago, your idea would've fallen by the wayside where brilliant ideas go to die. Bringing a new product to the market was incredibly risky and expensive. But that's all changed.

Today, it's easier than ever to test the market's want for that product for free and receive funding to bring it into the world.

Whether your product idea is a film, book, line of jewelry, nifty gadget, or lifesaving device, there are two companies that can help you get the money you need — provided the market thinks it's a good idea.

These companies are called **Kickstarter** and **Indiegogo**.

You've probably heard of them. They are a simple way to fund creative projects you resonate with — and get your own creative venture funded by like-minded people. You decide how much money you need, tell potential investors why you need it, and if you raise your requested amount, you get to use the money to develop your product.

The backers of projects, in return, will receive an agreed-upon gift. Normally the gifts range from a public 'thank you' if they pledge a few dollars to the full product if they pledge enough to cover the cost of production. It's your choice what gifts you'll give to your backers.

Kickstarter: www.kickstarter.com

Indiegogo: www.indiegogo.com

Starting a campaign is insanely simple. But executing a wildly successful campaign, in most cases, requires finesse.

Here's where you can gain that extra edge.

Tim Ferriss, author of *The 4-Hour Workweek* has posted a step-by-step explanation on how one entrepreneur raised $100,000 in 10 days to launch his project.

How to raise $100,000 in 10 days:

www.fourhourworkweek.com/2012/12/18/hacking-kickstarter-how-to-raise-100000-in-10-days-includes-successful-templates-e-mails-etc

Free Business Cards

Just getting your business off the ground? Try out premier printing company **MOO** for 50 free business cards. You can choose one of their 400 professionally designed templates, or make your own and upload photos from your computer or various social media websites.

MOO:

us.moo.com/uploader/?type=businesscard& promotional=1&ppid=659

Free Income Tax Preparation

If your adjusted gross income is under $58,000, you are eligible for the IRS' Free File software. The IRS partners with 14 major software companies who make their brand-name tax preparation software available for free to the public.

If you prefer having a human being to help you, Free File is also offered at select locations at **Volunteer Income Tax Assistance (VITA)** and **Tax Counseling for the Elderly (TCE)** programs.

Free File software:

apps.irs.gov/app/freeFile/jsp/wizard.jsp?ck

VITA and TCE programs in your area:

www.irs.gov/Individuals/Free-Tax-Return-Preparation-for-You-by-Volunteers

Free Credit Monitoring

If you're not already taking advantage of Credit Sesame, you've been missing out. Credit Sesame is a 100% FREE program you can use on your computer or your phone that offers you:

- Free monthly credit score
- Free credit monitoring and alerts
- Free analysis of all your credit cards and loans from an expert
- Free $50,000 identity theft insurance and ID restoration help.

It's like having a team of professional finance planners monitoring your financial health at all times — absolutely free. It's a no-brainer.

Credit Sesame: **www.creditsesame.com**

Free Trade Magazines

Doing business in today's hypercompetitive environment takes a commitment to staying ahead of the curve in your market.

What better way to do that than by subscribing to a trade magazine that keeps tabs on every leader, innovation, and idea that runs through it?

Sure, digging through to find the right one could get expensive. That's where **TradePub** can help. TradePub allows you to try out any of hundreds of trade magazines before you buy a single copy. No matter what industry you're in, you'll find a magazine that will bring you that extra advantage.

TradePub: www.tradepub.com

Get 70% More Interest From Your Checking Account

Regular savings accounts provide dismal interest rates. In fact, upon writing, the FDIC reports that the average rate is just 0.04%.

If you're unhappy with the amount of interest you're receiving, try out a FREE **Kasasa checking account**. With Kasasa, you could receive 3% interest and higher at financial institutions near you.

There are three catches to receiving the higher interest rates:

- **Have direct deposit of a paycheck** or other income once a month
- **Make a minimum of debit purchases** (10–15, normally)
- **Go paperless**. You must sign up for e-statements.

In return, you'll receive a 3% (or higher) APY on balances up to $10,000 for any month you meet all three criteria.

Other perks: No minimum balance to avoid fees. And with most accounts, they'll refund all ATM fees. Plus, you're FDIC or NCUA insured.

Where to find an account? Go to the link below and punch in your ZIP code. You'll find a list of financial institutions near you that offer these accounts.

Kasasa free checking:

www.kasasa.com/kasasa-providers/community-banking

Never Pay Another ATM Fee

How often have you found yourself *forced* to pay stupid ATM fees? Probably more times than you care to admit. Add them all up and you'd probably be horrified.

That's why you need to heed these little-known techniques to beating the fees and never get forced to pay another dime just for pulling money out.

First, **you could open a checking account at your brokerage house**.

Fidelity's Cash Management Account and **Schwab's High Yield Investor Checking** rebate all ATM fees, as long as you have a separate brokerage account. Ally Bank's online checking account customers pay no ATM fees. HSBC Direct will reimburse you up to three times per month.

Fidelity Cash Management:
www.fidelity.com/cash-management/
fidelity-cash-management-account/overview
Schwab's High Yield Investor Checking:
www.schwab.com/public/schwab/banking_
lending/checking_account
Ally Bank:
www.ally.com/bank/interest-checking-account

HSBC Direct:
www.us.hsbc.com/1/2/home/personal-banking

Or you could simply open a checking account at participating banks...

High-interest checking account customers at **EverBank** receive unlimited ATM fee reimbursements, provided their account balance exceeds $5,000. Same for **E-Trade Max-Rate** customers.

EverBank Checking:
www.everbank.com/banking/checking

E-Trade Max-Rate:
us.etrade.com/banking/checking-account

And always keep in mind that many places give cash back...

If there's a **Staples**, **Rite Aid**, **Walgreens**, **Whole Foods**, or **Best Buy** nearby, you can always pop in and get cash back. Keep in mind, though, there's normally a limit between $20–60.

And finally, you can join a credit union that uses **Allpoint**.

Many credit unions are part of a surcharge-free co-op network called Allpoint. They have 55,000 ATMs in their network, all free, as long as you use a credit union within their service.

Allpoint Network: www.allpointnetwork.com

Find one that fits your lifestyle and never pay ATM fees again.

Legally "Rob"
Credit Card Companies

There are many things that your credit card company wishes you'll never find out about. Especially if you're responsible with your credit cards and your credit score is excellent. Here are a few things to keep in mind that could save you thousands of dollars in the future.

They work for you. You have more power than they let on. Especially if you have a high credit score.

If you have over 700, you are in a good place to negotiate terms. Over 750? They're instructed to make sure you stick around at all costs.

*[NOTE: If you have poor credit, it's never too late to start repairing it. To do so, do what you can to **keep your balances low and your limits high**. Also, don't close out any credit card accounts if you don't have to, especially not all at once.]*

But even if your credit score isn't up there, you can still get them to bend over backward to keep you around.

LOWER YOUR CURRENT INTEREST RATES

Here's how you lower your interest rate on a high-rate card. Next time you get one of those credit card offers in the mail from a competitor, use it against your current provider. Call them (and remember, always be cordial) and tell them you're considering getting the new credit card so you can have a lower interest rate — even better if the provider is offering 0% APR on balance transfers for an extended period of time (Citi Bank's Simplicity card, for example, is currently offering 0% APR on balance transfers and purchases for 18 months). If your current rate is high enough, you'll spend less on the transfer fee (normally 3%) than you would in a month of interest. If that's the case, bring that up.

If the envelope from the competitor says "preapproved," tell them you're already approved, you just wanted to talk with them first. Also be sure to mention any other features the new card offers. Tell them you'd like to stay on their side, but are attracted to paying less in interest each month.

If you don't get anywhere with the customer service rep, ask to talk to a supervisor. Be polite, and don't get frustrated. Take note of the supervisor's name. If it doesn't work, call him or her back in a few months and try again — proving that you're worthy of their service by showing how responsible you've been. Or just put your money where your mouth is and switch.

To Beat the Annual Fee, Do This

The card issuer needs your business more than you need their credit card. If you're a U.S. citizen with decent credit, you're flush with attractive offers. Use this to your advantage.

Call the company you're interested in getting a card from and tell them you'd like to become a cardholder. *But*, you explain, you're looking at an offer from a competitor and the competitor's card has a lower interest rate or doesn't have an annual fee.

Ask them if they can beat the competitor's offer. If not, ask to talk to a supervisor and work your way up. The higher you go, the more willing they are to meet your needs.

If you already have a card that has an annual fee, you can beat it with this trick: Tell them you want to keep the card but you've found another card that's equally attractive without the annual fee (make sure you find that card... don't just bluff). Tell them that if they waive the fee, you'll stay on with them. If not, you'll consider cancelling the card altogether.

If you haven't used the card much, tell them you want to choose one of your cards to keep as your primary card. And if they waive the fee, you'll choose that one.

More often than not, if you play your cards right, they'll waive the fee.

Get Late Fees Removed and Keep Them From Reporting You

Many card issuers will tell you they don't report good customers for one offense. Don't take their word for it. As I mentioned in the travel section of this book, a late payment could knock off over 100 points from your credit score. That's a huge hit.

That's why you should always call them up and mention this promise (if they've made it somewhere online or to you personally). Then tell them honestly why you were late. As long as you're nice and honest, and late payments are a rare occurrence for you, there's a good shot they'll waive the fee and keep it from affecting your credit. Keep in mind when you call that you're not talking to big, evil banks. You're talking to humans who are likely willing to help people who appreciate their help.

Ask to Have Your Credit Limit Raised

Many people don't, but you can simply call your provider and ask to have your credit limit raised. Give them reasons why you deserve an increase. Is your job secure? Did you just get a raise recently? Never made a late payment?

If you succeed, it will give your credit score a nice boost because of the higher credit-to-debt ratio.

Be careful with this one... it could backfire. Only use this if you have a low balance and great payment history. Otherwise, they could take one look at your score and tell you they're going to have to lower your credit limit. This will, in turn, *lower* your credit score.

Get Debt Collectors Off Your Back

Debt collectors can, and will, try to intimidate you. Yes, you should pay off the debt you owe them, but don't let them scare you into doing it on their terms. Stay in control with these helpful tips:

Confront them head-on. What you resist persists... and nowhere does this ring more true than with debt collectors. When they call, demand they identify themselves appropriately. By law, they're not allowed to pose as law enforcement or say that they're from a government institution (which reportedly happens) — they have to tell you who they are and whom they work for. Also, they are required to inform you of your right to dispute the charge. And they have to work the dispute on your behalf, despite what they might tell you.

Download Consumer Finance's "Action Letters." ConsumerFinance.org has published five letters that you can use when replying to debt collectors. These letters will help you suss out any information about the claims being made against you and help protect you from inappropriate collection activities. You can download all of the letters at:

www.consumerfinance.gov/blog/debtcollection

Go to Ask Doctor Debt if you have any questions. You'll get access to what your rights are, what to expect, and how you can get the calls to stop.

If they're treating you wrong, don't hesitate to complain. The international trade association for debt collectors is listening. And chances are if you're driven to complain about a specific bill collector, you're probably not the first. Go to ACAInternational.org to submit a complaint.

Ask Doctor Debt: www.askdoctordebt.com

Debt collector trade association: www.ACAInternational.org

Action letter downloads:

www.consumerfinance.gov/blog/debtcollection

Stuff Your Bank Account
With Tax-Free Cash

If you're tired of watching state and federal taxes eat up all your profits, take advantage of these three opportunities to earn tax-free cash year after year.

Buy municipal bonds. Generally, state tax is not collected by people who reside in the same state where the bonds have been issued. So for instance, a bond issued in Massachusetts is exempt from Massachusetts state taxes.

To see what municipal bonds are available state by state, go here: www.municipalbonds.com

Check into an indexed universal life policy (IUL). An IUL is a form of universal life insurance that provides death benefit protection and allows you to "invest" your cash value in the overall stock market.

Sound risky? Many plans offer protection from downside risk — normally at 0%. If the stock market goes down, your cash value won't. That way, you can buy insurance and participate in the stock market with no downside.

Of course, there's a catch. Four of them, actually.

1. **The cash value isn't on par with your contributions.** Very little of your contributions go to your cash value in the first few years.

2. **The upside isn't limitless**. If you're in the midst of a raging bull market, you'll only get credit for it going up 12% that year, no matter how far it runs.

3. **You'll only receive a percentage of the market's performance**. This can range from 25–65%, but you'll never get 100%. Meaning, if the stock market goes up 10%, your cash value will rise 2.5–6.5%, depending on your plan.

4. **You're not guaranteed anything except what they tell you**. Your contract will likely have a guaranteed return. Check your contract thoroughly before you sign to see what they HAVE to pay you if all else fails.

When properly designed and managed, an IUL is a great way to grow your money tax-free.

Get the gift of giving. When you give away possessions or money, you do not have to pay taxes if it's a gift. You can give your children as much as $14,000 each without having to pay any taxes.

Outsource Your Financial Management — Free

Tired of losing track of where your money went? Talk to any successful person or organization, especially in finances, is likely central to their success.

If organizing your finances sounds overwhelming, don't worry. **Mint** has you covered. Just sign up and load in your financial information and they'll automatically track your finances, cent by cent. Not a single week will go by without you knowing precisely where your money is going.

That way, you'll know where you're spending too much, and in what places your money could be more useful and lucrative.

Oh, yeah, and it's FREE.

Simply log on to the Mint.com website to get started.

Mint: **www.mint.com**

Track Your Investments For Free

Having trouble keeping track of your portfolio? **Personal Capital** has you covered.

Their free investment tracking tool...

1. **Automatically links all of your investment accounts**, keeping your holdings updated second by second...
2. **Tracks all fees** you pay for each mutual fund or ETF.
3. **Provides detailed asset allocation graphs** for your entire portfolio.
4. **And automatically alerts you when your allocation is over- or underweight**, depending on your present tolerance for risk.

If this sounds good, visit the link and see it for yourself. Personal Capital FREE tool:

www.personalcapital.com/landing/registration

Pinpoint The Optimum Position For Your Social Security

Figuring out how to maximize your Social Security payments is tricky. That's why **AARP** created their free Social Security calculator.

It will show you why most people should wait as long as possible — and why a few people would be better off claiming earlier than usual.

Social Security Calculator:

www.aarp.org/work/social-security/social-security-benefits-calculator

Destroy The Sneaky Fees That Are Quietly Ruining Your Retirement

An AARP study found that 71% of 401(k) participants have no clue they're paying fees for their plans. What's scary is once it comes time to retire, these fees could cut up to 10% from your retirement fund.

Assume you have 35 years to retirement and have $25,000 in your 401(k). If your nest egg grows 7% and fees and expenses reduce that by 0.5 percent, your account balance will grow to $227,000 at retirement. Raise those fees to 1.5% and your account balance — in 35 years — will be $163,000. That 1% difference in fees reduces your retirement account by 28%.

In turn, it's in your best interest to set those fees as low as you can get them as soon as you possibly can.

What are these fees? How do you eradicate them?

First, you have administrative fees. This includes management fees, investment advisory fees, or account maintenance fees. If you're charged more than $50 per year, there are lower-cost 401(k) providers out there. Encourage your employer and your colleagues to seek out those lower-cost providers.

Second, asset-based fees. These fees are what you're required to pay to invest (you may know them as commissions or "loads"). They are to cover the transaction costs to buy mutual funds or any other investment. That number depends on the amount invested, what you're invested in, and the terms of your specific plan. In the latter, for example, insurance companies typically enforce an "asset charge" on top of the normal asset-based fees. To help minimize these fees from chipping chunks out of your retirement, request that your provider compile investments with the lowest fees for your consideration. Also see if your 401(k) allows for a "brokerage window." If it does, you'll be able to invest in mutual funds and other investments not included in the written plan. This way you'll be free to find lower-fee investments outside the confines of your agreement.

The third fee is the individual service fee. Those fees are couped when you use optional services within your 401(k), such as borrowing money, requesting checks, or even giving specific directions.

The more informed you are about these fees, the more you'll be able to whittle them down to a minimum. The following link will help:

www.dol.gov/ebsa/publications/401k_employee.html

Forget The Retirement Doom And Gloom

If "not having enough" for retirement keeps you up at night, get ready to sleep better than you have in ages.

Because of one explosive technology, one market expert predicts that in 20 years, you'll look back and see that you were part of the "luckiest generation that's ever lived."

The technology is what allows us to frack wells and pull oil out of shale.

Matt Insley is the market analyst who predicts it will create an economic boom unlike anything we've seen in our lives. He's managing editor of a free daily e-letter called *Daily Resource Hunter*. You can sign up at the link below.

Daily Resource Hunter:

www.dailyresourcehunter.com/sign-up

He and his colleague Byron King, award-winning editor and Harvard-trained geologist, have agreed to let you in on some of their most valuable stock picks to get into the shale boom.

DENBURY RESOURCES (NYSE: DNR)
CENOVUS ENERGY (NYSE: CVE)
HESS CORP. (NYSE: HES)

To get the latest on investing in resources, check out the *Daily Resource Hunter* today.

Daily Resource Hunter: www.dailyresourcehunter.com

Over 50? Don't Miss This!

Are you over 50 years old? If yes, consider yourself lucky.

There are currently over 2,000 programs that exist to help you pay for food, utilities, legal matters, health care, housing, and more. And **BenefitsCheckUp** wants to help you find all the ones that are right for you.

Just answer a few questions and then receive a personalized report that describes all the programs that are perfect for you.

BenefitsCheckUp: **www.benefitscheckup.org**

Trade Stocks With Zero Commissions

Have you considered firing your broker (and ridding yourself of all his fees)?

If paying the normal $5 or $10 for each trade is cutting into your profits, try out **Robinhood**.

Stanford grads Vladimir Tenev and Baiju Bhatt created Robinhood so you can trade as many stocks as you want — without fees. Their goal? "To make the public markets more available to more people," says Bhatt.

To see how it works, visit their website below.

Robin Hood: **www.robinhood.com**

Get Paid To Buy Stocks You Love

Motif lets you invest in intelligently designed baskets of stocks (called Motifs) based on trends or themes you're most interested in.

For example, let's say you want to invest in the biotech industry. You can buy into one motif called "Biotech Breakthroughs" and invest into a basket of 30 different biotech companies.

Some of the companies within this basket are focused on cancer drugs, others are looking to cure infectious diseases. Others specialize in autoimmune disorders, and a few more invest their time in research and diagnostics.

The best part of investing in a motif is you'll pay only one commission ($9.95) to get into up to 30 stocks.

Upon writing, the investment platform is offering a sweet deal. They're giving out up to $150 just for trying out their site. Perform one trade, you get $50. Three, you get $75. And five, you'll earn $150.

Again, each trade costs $9.95, so you'll get paid $100 just for investing in stocks you love.

Visit the links below to learn more on how Motif works, and to take advantage of their special deal while it lasts.

How Motif works:
www.motifinvesting.com/how-it-works/overview

Sign up for their special deal here:
www.motifinvesting.com/offers/150trade_090112

Chapter Twelve: Free Ways To Make Money

Claim Free Money Today

First things first. Collect all the money owed to you. If the government or a company owes you money, it becomes part of an unclaimed database. They're not going to come knocking on your door begging you to take it. You have to go find it.

According to an article released from NPR, the federal government alone is sitting on $18 billion in unclaimed funds. Unfortunately, the government doesn't have just one single database to search through all of the different factions. Instead, you'll need to visit each separately and search on your own.

Here are all the links you'll need:

Search your state's listing: www.unclaimed.org

Unclaimed pensions from former employers: search.pbgc.gov/mp

Unclaimed tax refunds:
www.irs.gov/uac/Does-the-IRS-Have-Money-Waiting-For-You%3F

Search the FDIC for unclaimed funds from bank failures: www2.fdic.gov/funds/index.asp

Use this link to search through credit union failures: www.ncua.gov/Resources/AM/Pages/UnclaimedDeposits.aspx

Search through the Securities and Exchange Commission (SEC) claims funds to see if a company or person owes you, an investor, money:

www.sec.gov/divisions/enforce/claims.htm

Search for unclaimed matured savings bonds at the Treasury: www.treasuryhunt.gov

For all foreign claims, visit this link:

www.fms.treas.gov/tfc/index.html

Be A Taskrabbit

There are several sites you can use to do small tasks for people in your community. Anyone can outsource their chores, errands, and tasks to anyone else who is willing to do them. TaskRabbit is one of the more well-known sites, but far from the only one. Also, it's free to sign up.

TaskRabbit: www.taskrabbit.com
Fancy Hands: www.fancyhands.com
Agent Anything: www.agentanything.com
Gigwalk: www.gigwalk.com

Make Money Doing
Whatever You Want

When Micha Kaufman set out to launch his business in early 2010, he wanted to create a place where anyone could make money from their talents — no matter what those talents were. "Today, everyone has a talent that someone else needs," he said in an interview with *U.S. News & World Report*. "[We thought], How cool would it be to put these amazing talents together in one place?'"

Out of that one question emerged a website called **Fiverr.com.**

Fiverr is 100% free to join. And it's a place where anyone can sell their talent online to anyone in the world **for as little as $5 to as much as $500 per task**.

Fiverr has become insanely popular in large part due to how easy their site is to use. It's incredibly easy for users to buy and sell quickly. Depending on the difficulty of their task, you could perform multiple tasks in three or four hours a day and still pull in a nice income.

Here's just one example of hundreds: Mark Mason, a semi retired publicist living in Chicago, started writing email and marketing materials on Fiverr. In no time, he was earning $150–300 a day working only three–four hours. That income alone allowed him to buy a new home in Indiana.

Below I've listed several skills that are currently in high demand. If you have any of these skills, consider yourself lucky and jump on Fiverr immediately.

Video production: Creating intro videos, editing existing videos, etc.

Graphic design: banners, simple logos, book covers, and more.

Tutoring: Know something that lots of people want to learn (different language, especially proficient in math, science, history, etc.)? Offer up 15-minute phone or Skype calls to answer any questions.

Voiceovers: Have a radio voice? Create commercials, client videos, and more.

For more examples, visit this link:
www.slideshare.net/juliefletcher123/top-10-things-to-sell-on-fiverr?related=1&utm_campaign=related&utm_medium=1&utm_source=3

Even if you don't have any specific skills, the possibilities for you are endless.

For example, here's one bizarre (somewhat of a) success story:

One man who goes by the alias **ShoeNice** has made at least $595 on Fiverr by eating one piece of paper per $5 order. That's right... he gets paid to eat paper.

We don't recommend you eat 119 pieces of paper, but this goes to show... you can make money doing about anything, as long as your customers want it. No specific skills necessary.

See for yourself.

Fiverr: **www.fiverr.com**

Loan Stuff You Don't Use

The next time you check out your garage, closet, or attic, take note of how much useful stuff is just gathering dust. Then go to **Loanables** to see how much money you could be making each week by renting this stuff out.

Not only is Loanables a great way make a little cash, it's also a wonderful way to meet more people living in your community.

Below are links for Loanables and a price-comparison chart so you know what's a fair price to rent your belongings for.

Loanables: www.loanables.com

Price comparison chart:

www.loanables.com/misc/comparative_pricing.pdf

Get Paid To Exercise

Nexercise is an iPhone app that will pay you to exercise. Well, you'll get the chance to get paid. The more you exercise, the more likely you are to win from a pool of fellow exercisers.

Nexercise: **www.nexercise.com**

GymPact uses cash stakes to help you achieve your fitness goals. The difference between GymPact and Nexercise is you earn money by sticking to your goals, paid for by others who fail to meet their own goals.

Need motivation? Check out GymPact.

GymPact: **www.gym-pact.com**

Sell Your Smartphone Pictures

Take a lot of pictures on your iPhone? Sell them for cash! iPhone app **Foap** makes it simple to earn $5 each time someone downloads your image from their website. Best part, each image can be downloaded multiple times. So if you take great pictures, you could make good money from each one.

Foap: www.foap.com

What if I know nothing about photography? Don't worry. Massachusetts Institute of Technology (MIT) is offering a world-class photojournalism class for free.

Free MIT Course:

ocw.mit.edu/courses/writing-and-humanistic-studies/21w-749-documentary-photography-and-photojournalism-still-images-of-a-world-in-motion-spring-2009/index.htm

Make Money On Things You Already Buy

Here's a clever way to make money on things you were going to buy anyway. You're going to need a friend with an Amazon account for this one.

You probably know... you can get nearly anything on Amazon. And most of it you can get shipped to your house for free. Next time you think of going to the local store to buy something, check on Amazon first.

And when you buy those things on Amazon (oftentimes cheaper than you would retail), you could be making some of that money back.

In fact, you can earn up to 15% each time you purchase something from Amazon, no matter what it is.

Here's how...

First step, have a friend or family member sign up for the affiliate program. It's free to sign up. You just have to already have an account.

Amazon's affiliate program:

affiliate-program.amazon.com/gp/associates/
promo/affiliate-programs.html

Second step, after you've signed up, it's time to build links on their affiliate account for things you plan to buy on Amazon.

By "build links," I mean create affiliate links so that when you use them to buy products on Amazon, you'll make a commission. Each product will need its own link.

Remember: You're creating these links in your friend's account.

Sound complicated? Don't worry, Amazon makes it simple. They'll walk you through it in the link below.

Creating affiliate links:

affiliate-program.amazon.com/gp/associates/ promo/buildlinks.html

Whenever you click your custom link and buy the product, your friend's account will receive a commission.

Third step, you and your friend split the profits!

[NOTE: Double your profits by doing the same thing for your friend. That way, you'll both have accounts with money flowing into them each week.]

Get Cash Back For Your Already-Bought Groceries

Forget extreme couponing. Unless you're clipping coupons full time, you'll never have enough time to get the kinds of deals you might see on TV. Luckily, **Ibotta** makes getting cash for your groceries as simple as possible.

All you have to do is go on their website and browse for offers for the products you want to buy. Then, after you've bought your items at the grocery store, just scan your receipt. Within hours, money will show up in your account that you can withdrawal (with PayPal) whenever you want!

Moreover, Ibotta works for more than just groceries. You can use it at select restaurants and retail stores, for the latest gadgets, at pet stores, and more.

Ibotta: **www.ibotta.com**

Get Paid To Share Your Opinion

What if you could make a dollar a minute telling people what you think? **Google** has made it possible.

Answer quick surveys and earn $1.00 in credits for each survey you complete. Some questions include, "Which logo is best?" and "Which promotion is most compelling?"

Each survey normally takes only one–five minutes.

Google Opinion Rewards: play.google.com/store/apps/details?id=com.google.android.apps.paidtasks

More Ways to Get Paid for Your Opinion

Join the 20/20 research panel. Companies pay top dollar to hear what consumers have to say about their products. The 20/20 panel is your fast track to connecting with these companies, telling them what you think, and getting paid.

www.2020panel.com

Help out Harvard. Participate in Harvard studies online and make an average of $25 per session:

www.hbs.edu/cler

Get paid to visit websites. UserTesting.com will pay you $10 a pop to visit websites and give your honest feedback.

www.usertesting.com

Turn Your House Into A Cash Machine

Own your own home? If so, there are hundreds of ways you can start making money TODAY using what you already have. Let's go through just a few of the ways...

Rent Extra Space

Have a closet you don't use? What about a little space in the attic or garage? Put it up for rent! You can get paid to hold onto other people's stuff. And **Store at My House** makes it super simple. There's no fee to post your space... you set the price... and they provide free sample contracts for you to use to streamline the side business.

Store at My House: www.storeatmyhouse.com

Rent Your Driveway

Have an extra spot in the driveway? Yep. You can rent that too. Just visit **Park at My House** for more information on how.

Park at My House: www.parkatmyhouse.com

Rent Your Backyard

Not only does **Airbnb** make it easy for you to rent a room or your entire house, you can also rent your backyard to potential campers passing through.

Airbnb: www.airbnb.com

Rent Your Home Tax-Free (Or Live Rent-Free)

Most people don't know this, but you're legally allowed to rent your home for 14 days or less and not pay a cent of taxes on the money you earn.

And fortunately, there's an easy, relatively risk-free way of renting your home.

You may've heard of the company. It's called **Airbnb**. It takes a few minutes to sign up and list your home. Then, all you need to do is take a few snapshots, upload them, and you're done!

You get to choose who you let rent out your place, and you can "vet" them based on past reviews of other places they've stayed.

Also, if you have an extra room and don't mind renting it out every so often, you could live rent or mortgage-free year round on the money you earn.

Airbnb: **www.airbnb.com**

[NOTE: Couple this secret with those you learned in the Travel section of this book and you could get paid to go on vacation!]

Chapter Thirteen:
Personal

Get Treated Like A VIP Wherever You Go

Get an upgrade next time you check into a hotel. Get a key to the concierge floor. Get a fruit basket in your room when you arrive. Get a seat in first class… and maybe even a blanket.

VIP treatment isn't just for rock stars. It's for you, too… as long as you play by the rules.

RULE #1: DRESS NICE AND BE NICE.

When you look good, and make other people feel good, it's a deadly combination. Also, be forgiving to anyone whose job it is to help you. All VIPs have to wait sometimes — those who deal with it gracefully and with class are normally those who remain on the lists.

RULE #2: USE THE LAW OF RECIPROCITY.

If you've ever been handed a limp daisy from a Hare Krishna, you know the power of reciprocity. You feel compelled, obligated even, to repay the favor. So you slip him a crumpled up dollar and scamper off before he tries anything else.

Rather than resenting this tactic, you should use it to your advantage.

Bring along something nice to give out when the opportunity presents itself. Something cheap. My colleague once told me about a friend's wife who always becomes buddies with her hotel and airport clerks — especially if something goes wrong. She makes sure to give them little 5-cent mints or chocolates. It's no surprise, then, that she's always first in line to receive an upgrade over any other customers.

RULE #3: ASK FOR WHAT YOU WANT AND NEVER SETTLE FOR STANDARD.

If you want an upgrade, you're not going to get it if you don't ask for it. If you want first class, the clerks aren't going to hand it to you without you first expressing interest. The people who get the best rooms in hotels do one of two things:

A) They ask for them

B) They pay out the woo-ha for them

Many people are uncomfortable asking for a better room. It's not surprising, then, when they are "forced" to settle for subpar rooms next to the elevators, with little light or with a terrible view.

RULE #4: DON'T BOOK THROUGH AN ONLINE DISCOUNT SITE.

If you find a great price through an online hotel discount website (Hotels.com, Hotwire.com, Expedia.com, etc.) ask the hotel to match the price. They probably will. Don't talk to the general manager. Talk to someone who speaks the language of money: the sales manager. They're more likely to see the benefit of price matching, whereas the general manager is more likely to focus on principle, or how they shouldn't give guests preferential treatment.

So you've done that and got a good deal. Now keep this ball rolling. Use the fifth rule now...

RULE #5: DON'T BE AFRAID TO NAMEDROP

When you go to check in, always name-drop the sales or

general manager. Then, if you're not satisfied with your current room, ask for an upgrade. For example, a little before you ask for that upgrade, you could say, "If you see (name) today, can you tell him that (your name) said thanks again?" It takes some finesse to get right, but name-dropping, when done artfully, is infinitely powerful.

RULE #6: JOIN ALL THE LOYALTY PROGRAMS. You don't have to go to one hotel over and over in order to enjoy perks anymore. The market is flooded with loyalty programs, and that has pushed hotels to stack perk on top of perk to keep up with the competition. Just for signing up for many free loyalty cards, you can take advantage of these perks (free Wi-Fi, free upgrades, free nights) — even if you've never stayed a night in that hotel before.

RULE #7: LET SOMEONE ELSE RESERVE YOUR TABLE FOR YOU.

When you plan your next dinner out, one company, called OpenTable, wants to take care of the dirty work for you. With just a few taps on your smartphone, they'll make sure you have the best table available at over 30,000 restaurants worldwide.

The more you use their service, the more points you earn. These points can redeemed for "Dining Cheques" that work like cash at participating restaurants.

OpenTable: www.opentable.com

RULE #8: BE "THE AMBASSADOR".

Once you start to frequent a place, become "the ambassador."

What does that mean, exactly? Become the person who talks, and connects to, everyone in the place.

Remember everyone's names, details of their lives, and go in sometimes on an off-night and chat them up.

This will go a long way the next time you want to impress friends, a business partner, or a date in the future. Just take them to one of your "ambassador" spots and watch their astonishment as you both get preferential treatment.

RULE #9: TELL A SECRET

Everyone loves secrets. We all love to be "in the know." By sharing something personal or private with another person, something you've "never told anyone before," you create a trust and sense of obligation that wouldn't exist otherwise.

"Off the record, I think you should know..."

"I shouldn't be telling you this, but..."

RULE #10: MAKE "VALUE COMPLIMENTS"

Compliments, when executed correctly, are extremely powerful. They are like seeds that will grow into something greater, benefiting both the complimenter and –tee.

The trick is to give people compliments based on someone's values, and not based on superficial things like eyes, hair, clothes, etc.

Superficial compliments are a dime a dozen. They only scratch the surface of making someone feel unique and special. Value compliments, though, are a collector's item.

So how do you know what to say?

Sussing out what someone values is simple: Just pay attention to what makes them excited. What do they take pride in? Take note and use it genuinely and appropriately.

For example, if you notice someone prides themselves on being a loyal friend, maybe you could tell them that.

"You're clearly an amazing friend."

If that's a little too obvious, try this...

"You're obviously a really great listener."

Talking to someone who always tells stories about their kids?

"You seem like a really great mother/father."

Use the rules wisely (and genuinely) and you'll be first in line for those VIP perks wherever you find yourself.

Get Your Way Without Saying A Word

Psychologists will tell you that 60–80% of all communication is nonverbal. Most people, though, put little to no thought into what messages they're sending with their bodies.

No matter what message you want to send, there's a way to do so without even saying a word.

For example...

LEADERS nonverbally encourage others to follow them with their body language. The name of this game is "puffing" yourself up without exaggerating it. Humans are still animals, and many things that work in the wild still work on our unconscious.

Start first by claiming your territory. Spread yourself out to make yourself as big as possible without looking absurd. When you stand, hold your arms slightly away from your body, and your feet slightly apart. When you sit in a shared space, spread your materials out slightly farther than the width of your shoulders.

Signal confidence and control with your hands by spreading your fingers wide when you make hand gestures.

Look calm and collected even when you don't feel it by telling this to yourself just before you face a potentially diffi-cult situation:

I may face problems. But even if there is yelling and screaming,

I am going to transcend it. I have a responsibility and a right to be calm and to help others remain calm.

Telling yourself this will raise the odds that you'll remain calm. Having a cool demeanor is important.

People gravitate toward people who can keep their cool in difficult situations. They tend to avoid those who seem like they could fall into a panic.

Be Confident

People trust what confident people say, and the signals you send to others largely determine whether or not you're in that "camp."

Steeple those digits. Touch your fingertips together with your fingertips pointed up and spread wide. Studies have shown that jurors are more likely to believe testimony when the witness uses the steeple.

Enter rooms without hesitation. Walking into a room without hesitation shows that you believe in yourself — and others should too. If you hesitate, others may assume you have an uncertain temperament and might place less value on your words.

Keep that chin up. It's more than just an expression. Holding up your chin shows you're confident enough to expose the most vulnerable spot on your body: your neck.

Look Like a Friend

Lift those eyebrows. Whenever you see someone you want to be friends with, arch your eyebrows. Raising your eyebrows is a signal of openness and attraction. When you let someone see more of your eyes, you're showing them you have nothing to hide.

Avoid face-to-face conversations. People will feel more comfortable and connected if you are at a right angle of them, or by their side. Face-to-face implies confrontation and is too personal. Also, point your feet (and legs, if you cross them) in the direction of the person you're speaking to.

These are only a few examples of hundreds you can use to enhance every single interaction you have each day. To learn more, check out the FREE body language dictionary by following the link below.

Body language dictionary:

www.bodylanguageproject.com/dictionary

Lose 15 Pounds of Ugly Fat For Free

Struggling with your weight? Don't get ripped off by companies that are full of hype but never deliver the goods. Forget all the diet pills and cleanses. Here's a FREE way to lose up to 15.5 pounds in three months — with minimal to no exercise.

Simply drink two 8-ounce glasses of water right before each meal. Not only will this boost your digestion and metabolism, it'll also help fill your stomach to prevent overeating.

Many people confuse thirst with hunger, often feeling hungry when their body is really asking for hydration. Symptoms of dehydration (feeling weak, dizzy, and cranky) mimic those of hunger and contribute to this confusion.

Drinking two glasses of water before each meal will also help cleanse your body of excess waste — dropping more weight out of your body.

If you want to lose even more, do these things to add an extra kick.

Replace soda with water and lemon. If you're drinking sugary drinks, stop. Instead, drink lemon water if you need some kind of flavor. Not only is it refreshing, the pectins in lemons help reduce food cravings.

Drink it ice cold. Drinking ice cold water helps to boost your metabolism. Your body has to work harder to warm the water up, burning more calories.

Walk. Walking controls weight, blood sugar, and cholesterol levels. The heart and lungs grow more efficient with a regular walking regimen due to an increase in blood circulation. Walking relieves depression, anxiety, and stress by producing endorphins. It can stimulate thinking. The risk of injury is low. And it's simple to do.

Avoid white carbs. That's bread, rice, cereal, potatoes, pasta, and any fried foods. These foods will make you pack on weight faster than any other.

Eat the same meals (K.I.S.S). People who lose the most weight are normally those who keep their diets within a simple framework and stick to it. Here's a simple guideline of foods that can help you lose weight with moderate exercise.

Proteins:

Egg whites with one whole egg for flavor
Chicken breast or thigh
Grass-fed organic beef
Pork

Legumes:

Lentils
Black beans
Pinto beans

Vegetables:

Spinach
Asparagus
Peas
Mixed vegetables

Want to kick up your weight-loss goal a notch? How does losing 20 pounds of fat in 30 days sound?

Here's how author Tim Ferriss did it, and how you can do it too: **www.fourhourworkweek.com/2007/04/06/how-to-lose-20-lbs-of-fat-in-30-days-without-doing-any-exercise/**

*[NOTE: Couple these tips with our **Get Paid to Exercise** secret to lose weight and earn money! See table of contents.]*

Make Your Brain Run Faster And Stronger

Despite what you might've been taught to believe, no matter what age you are, your brain is constantly changing. Meaning, you always have the opportunity to improve your IQ, visual acuity, and ability to manage and process data... skills we equate to being "smart."

Here are some simple — and 100% free — tricks to boost your brainpower.

Have more sex. Princeton scientists studied a group of sexually active rats, comparing them with rats who were having sex only a couple times a month. They found that the more active rats had an increased number of neurons in their brains, especially in the regions responsible for controlling memory. They also grew more cells in their brains — and had more connections between those cells — than the less sexually active rats. They believe this finding may hold true in humans due to the lower levels of stress hormones found in people who have more sex.

Avoid sugar. "Eating a high-fructose diet," Fernando Gomez-Pinilla, a professor of neurosurgery at UCLA, said in an interview, "over the long term alters your brain's ability to learn and remember information."

In an experiment with rats, Fernando's team fed one group

a sugary diet and another a healthy diet for six weeks. After six weeks, the rats fed the sugary diet were slower and their brains had declined. Good news: Eating nuts and salmon can counteract this disruption.

Play video games. You know, those things your kids or grandkids are always sticking their nose in. You'll get more out of it than just improved hand-eye coordination. Researchers in Belgium did an MRI analysis on 150 teenagers. Those who played video games frequently had more brain cells in the left ventral striatum — the part responsible for controlling emotions and behavior. The more developed this region is, the better you learn. Plus, you'll have the added benefit of bonding with your kids or grandkids.

Drink plenty of water. When your body is dehydrated, your brain literally shrinks away from your skull. Scary. Also, a U.K. study showed that brains had to work much harder on fairly simple tasks when low on water. Stay hydrated.

Take up swimming or yoga. Yoga and swimming improve the blood flow to your brain, bringing with it more oxygen. The more oxygen your brain receives, the stronger and healthier it becomes.

Just walk. Forty minutes of walking three times a week can drastically improve your memory and intelligence by improving the connectivity between cells and your nervous system.

Expand your circle. When psychologists at University College London scanned the brains of 125 college students and looked at their Facebook accounts, they found something interesting. The students with the most friends also had significantly larger brains, especially in the areas of memory and emotional response.

Spa Treatments On The House

When Melissa Broughton walks into a spa, she's treated like a part of the royal family. In Hawaii, for example, she sauntered into Halele'a Spa and received a scalp massage, aromatherapy, reflexology, a lomilomi four-handed massage, and a facial — all for free.

"If that wasn't dreamy enough," she wrote in an article explaining how she did it, "many of the spas I visit are resort spas or connected with a boutique hotel. The PR managers of these properties feel it necessary that I 'experience' all of the accommodations to write a thorough review of their spa. So they often offer me free nights in their hotels as well."

If you're not brimming with jealousy yet, this might tip you over the edge: **She gets PAID $200 or more each time she visits a spa**.

Sound too good to be true? It did to her at first.

In her words: "I used to think it was too good to be true until I started writing reviews for spas and spa treatments. Now not only do I get complimentary 'signature' treatments (usually the best, longest, and most expensive on the spa menu), but I'm also being paid to write an article about my experience."

All she has to do is write a short article about her experience.

In return, she receives the most luxurious spa treatments money can buy, all for free.

Think you need special writing experience or connections to get paid to be pampered? According to Melissa, you can think again.

"Yes," Melisa said, "I'm a travel writer specializing in writing about spas. But previous travel writing experience is not a prerequisite to getting paid to write spa reviews or getting these sorts of perks. Anybody can get in on the action."

First, find all the magazines and websites that publish articles about spas.

Second, do your research. Look over the content and write down the proper contact information.

And third, write about previous spa experiences you've had.

Once you've done that, head over to Melissa's article to see how you can turn this article into free days at some of the world's top spas.

Spa treatments on the house:
www.thebarefootwriter.com/2012/02/writing-your-way-to-luxurious-spa-treatments-on-the-house

Free Health Services

If you need a little help with eye care or dental exams, a couple organizations have you covered.

Organizations like **InfantSEE.org** and **EyeCareAmerica. org** can provide you with free eye exams.

Similarly, **Dentistryfromtheheart.org** offers free dental exams to current and new customers. Visit their website for more details.

InfantSEE: www.infantsee.org

EyeCare America: www.eyecareamerica.org

Dentistry From The Heart: www.dentistryfromtheheart.org

Save Up To $2,000 On Prescription Drugs THis Year

Spending too much on your prescriptions? Follow these simple steps and save up to $2,000 on your prescriptions this year.

First, if you haven't already, sign up for an AARP membership. They have fantastic discounts on most prescription drugs available at pharmacies. You can save as much as 38% off of each drug. You can check out the details at aarphealthcare.com.

AARP health care: **www.aarphealthcare.com**

You can also get an RXRelief Card for free at rxreliefcard. com. It gives you at least 75% discount on all prescription drugs available at pharmacies. More than 50,000 pharmacies recognize the RXRelief card.

RX Relief: **www.rxreliefcard.com**

Stick to the generics. The bigger the brand, the more expensive the medicine. Nearly every generic pill has the exact chemical makeup as those big-name counterparts.

Get samples. Simply ask your doctor for samples. Sometimes, you'll get so many samples that they can last more than a month. That saves you a lot of money.

Make sure there is a review of the drug being given to you. This will help you get a coupon that will give you a discount. This will allow you to save up to $200.

Go rural. Urban pharmacies are more likely to have higher prices than rural ones. *Consumer Reports* found that a month's supply of generic Actos cost $203 in Raleigh, North Carolina, whereas outside of the city, it cost only $37.

Save Up To 80% On Your Health Care

If you haven't heard the term "medical tourism," you're missing out on a huge opportunity to save incredible amounts of money on your health care.

Medical tourism is where a citizen of one country travels to another to receive medical, dental, and surgery care for far cheaper — often with better care.

Despite all the cautionary tales of traveling to dangerous nations with germ-infested hospitals and untrained surgeons... millions of Americans have saved billions of dollars traveling to foreign countries for world-class surgery or dental work. That's right. They're are getting the same quality of treatment (sometimes better) for up to 70% off.

[NOTE: And if you couple this with our FREE TRAVEL secrets, you'll be able to get your airfare and accommodation for free! See above.]

Take a look at the cost comparison chart on the following page.

To learn more, visit the Medical Tourism Association's website below.

Medical Tourism Association:

www.medicaltourismassociation.com

Or you can speak to our in-house medical tourism expert and co-founder of MedRetreat, Judd Anglin. He'd be happy to answer any of your questions regarding the process and costs. His email address is janglin@lfb.org.

MedRetreat: www.medretreat.com

PROCEDURE	COST IN U.S.	COST ABROAD
Orthopedic		
Hip Replacement	$40,000–$65,000	$7,000–$13,000
Hip Resurfacing	$50,000–$60,000	$8,000–$12,000
Knee Replacement	$45,000–$80,000	$7,500–$12,000
Neurology		
Spinal Fusion	$80,000–$100,000	$5,000–$10,000
Spinal Disc Replacement	$100,000–$150,000	$8,000–$12,000
Discectomy	$20,000–$24,000	$5,000–$7,000
Cardiology		
Angioplasty	$50,000–$65,000	$5,000–$7,000
Heart Bypass	$90,000–$120,000	$10,000–$18,000
Heart Valve Replacement	$125,000–$175,000	$13,000–$18,000
Gynecology		
Hysterectomy	$18,000–$25,000	$4,000–7,000
Cosmetic		
Face & Neck Lift	$8,000–$15,000	$2,500–$4,000
Breast Augmentation	$6,000–$12,000	$3,500–$5,000
Tummy Tuck	$5,000–$12,000	$3,800–$5,200
Liposuction/Area	$2,000–$3,000	$800–$1,200
Dental		
Dental Implants/Tooth	$3,000–$5,000	$800–$2,000
Dental Crowns	$800–$1,200	$200–$600

Free Household Items

Before you head out to a department store, check out **Freecycle**.

Freecycle is a simple way for communities to give away stuff they no longer want. You don't even have to sign up to see what people in your area have to offer.

And of course, if you have anything that needs to be hauled off, try it out!

Freecycle: **www.freecycle.com**

(Nearly) Free Air Conditioning

Today you'll learn how to keep your place cool for far less than you're paying now. How? Build your own air conditioner with parts lying around your garage.

A do-it-yourself air conditioner is cheap and simple to construct and could save you hundreds of dollars each year on your AC bill.

The Good Survivalist has you covered with five different designs to choose from. Hop over to their site and start building.

The Good Survivalist:

www.thegoodsurvivalist.com/5-easy-to-make-homemade-air-conditioners-that-will-save-you-200-per-month-on-your-ac-bill-and-keep-you-frosty-cool-all-summer

Free Emergency Electricity

If your power ever goes out, which at some point it will, don't just sit there and rely on batteries until the utility company saves you. Here's a way you can have enough power to charge a mobile device or a radio to keep you safe and informed — in case of an emergency.

This secret has to do with a secret power source in your home that's always live, even during blackouts. I'm talking about that phone jack right under your nose.

You probably noticed that nearly every time the power goes out, the landlines are still up and running. That's because the phone company maintains their own backup power system, and all the power the phone needs comes from them. Even when the phone isn't in plugged in, a constant DC signal of about 50–60 volts runs through your phone jack.

Today, you're going to learn how to use that underutilized electricity... even if you don't currently have a landline service set up.

There are five (somewhat) simple steps to follow. For step-by-step instructions and an instructional video, visit the link below.

Emergency power:

www.instructables.com/id/How-to-Get-Emergency-Power-from-a-Phone-Line/?ALLSTEPS

Free Plants And Trees

Do you have a green thumb? Here's how to create a beautiful, lush garden in your backyard — absolutely free.

Contact Local Landscape Firms

Many landscape firms have a problem of excess plants and yard waste. And normally, they're forced to pay fees to get rid of it all. I'm sure most would be glad to have someone come and pick it up rather than have it dumped.

All you have to do is contact landscape firms in your area and either ask them specifically for what you want. Tell them you'll pick it up. The easier you make it for them, the more likely they are to agree.

Some will tell you no right off the bat. Don't get discouraged, and keep trying.

Post Wanted Ads

Freecycle and **Craigslist** are the perfect platforms for seeing if anyone around you has plants to give away. Simply sign up to either and post a short and sweet ad like this one:

WANTED

I'll be more than happy to come to you and take any extra plants off your hands. Please let me know if I can help you in your garden in exchange. I'm not afraid of hard work!

Contact me at
(*put email address here*).

10 Free Trees (When You Sign Up)

Become an **Arbor Day Foundation** member and have free seeds sent to your home. Membership cost is $10 for six months.

Arbor Day Foundation: www.arborday.org

Check Your Local Nursery

All nurseries have to at some point get rid of the plants that aren't selling well to make room for those that do. Oftentimes, that means throwing them out. Check with your local nurseries and let them know you're interested in any potential throwaways.

Free Seeds

If you're looking for free seeds, look no further than **WinterSown**.

WinterSown is a nonprofit organization that provides seed and growing information to individuals, schools, and groups.

They also offer free seeds to anyone who wants them. Upon writing, they have three offers:

Six Pack of Seeds: A variety of six different sample-size packs.

Tomato Seeds: Select the varieties of tomato seeds you want out of nearly 150.

Group Seed Requests: Connect with WinterSown members and see if they have the seeds you need.

WinterSown's Free Seeds:

www.wintersown.org/wseo1/Free_Seeds.html

Chapter Fourteen: Invest Like The Elite

Pay The IRS What They Deserve

Ever wish you could keep from paying Uncle Sam even a nickel come tax time?

Aside from taking a huge pay cut, there's another way to pay little to no taxes: Make your income equal your itemized deductions.

If you're a single filer, your standard deduction is $5,950. Married? It's around $12,000.

Make $5,950 a year... no taxes. If you're retired and not pulling in little income, that's all you need to know.

I assume, though, your situation is probably different.

To show you how to cut your taxes down to ribbons, we've enlisted the help of Sandy Botkin. He's the author of *Lower Your Taxes — Big Time!* and he's our in-house tax expert.

Here's his take...

Start a Home-Based Business

First, Sandy recommends you take a look at another great mass movement in the United States (alongside the **Economy 2.0** mentioned elsewhere in this book): the home-based business.

There are two tax systems you can choose to be a part of — one for the employee and another for small/home-based business owners.

Being a part of the small/home-based business is much better than the former. Why?

"In addition to the tax deductions employees can get," Sandy writes, "small business people can deduct, with proper documentation, their house, their spouses (by hiring them), their business vacations, their cars, and food with colleagues. They can also set up a pension plan that makes any government plan seem paltry in comparison and deduct most of their "vacation" trips if they combine them with an appropriate amount of business."

[NOTE: Don't know what type of business to start? Check out the Table of Contents for Chapter Thirteen on Free Ways to Make Money. Inside, you'll learn many ways to start a business for free, right from the comfort of your own home.]

Here are the things you can write off as a home-based business owner.

Deduct Your Fun

According to Sandy, you can deduct your fun and audit-proof your records. As of writing, no receipts are needed for entertainment expenses under $75 per expense.

Here's all the fun you can deduct:

- Theater tickets, golf, plays, and other associated entertainment
- Season tickets
- Home entertainment
- Small and large parties
- Lunches for employees
- And more.

Moving along, here's another trick you can use with a home-based business.

The Income Shift Secret of the Wealthy

This little-known trick is called "income shifting." It's one of the wealthiest's best-kept secrets.

Here's what you do... and all the benefits you'll receive:

- **Hire your spouse** and save a bundle deducting medical expenses
- **Hire your son or daughter** and deduct the equivalent of their education and weddings
- **Gift property to a person in a lower tax bracket and sell it**. This way, you can pay the tax at their bracket
- **Double-deduct all your equipment** plus protect it from judgments.

[NOTE: As a Laissez Faire Club *member, you have free access to our* Vanishing Point *report. Inside this report, you'll learn how to "disappear" from the IRS and save a boatload of money. Simply log onto our website at lfb.org and go to the "Reports" section.*

Here's the direct link:

www.lfb.org/reports/the-vanishing-point-how-to-disappear-from-the-irs-this-tax-season-and-save-a-boatload-of-money-in-the-process

To learn even more about Sandy Botkin's little-known tax strategies, check out his book Lower Your Taxes — Big Time!*]*

Warren Buffett's Foolproof Tax Strategy

If you're not investing in the strategy you'll learn here, you're missing out on swaths of the easiest income you'll ever make — tax-free.

Let me explain...

Warren Buffett likes to point out that his tax rate is less than that of the people who clean his office at night — all because of his dividend income.

But Buffett isn't investing in normal dividends...

He's investing in what Agora Financial's income expert Neil George calls "Elite Dividends."

Investing in Elite Dividends

In 2008, Neil wrote to his readers in his *Income on Demand* newsletter, Investors started running for the hills at such a rate it could only be compared to 1929:

Yet one investor took his own contrarian advice seriously. *The New York Times* reported this in 2009: When so many others were running scared last autumn, Mr. Buffett invested billions in Goldman Sachs — and got a far better deal than Washington. He then staked billions more on General Electric.

Boy, did he ever!

Goldman and GE were two companies hit hard by the

recession that started in 2008. They both lost more than 50% in a matter of months. Dividends in these firms began to look scary. GE even cut its payments by two-thirds shortly after its stock collapse. So how did Buffett fare? Like no one else...

While both of these companies were diluting their common shareholder base, and even slashing dividends, Buffett was able to lock in double-digit yields, plus extra guarantees through investments we call Elite Dividends.

Both of these deals were privately made between the companies' boards and Buffett. Goldman's elite dividends gave him special rights to 10% yields indefinitely, on top of a right to buy $5 billion worth of common stock for $115 per share at any time over the next five years.

GE's elite dividends gave Buffett another lucrative set of rights. First, he receives an indefinite 10% yield — like the GS one. On top of that, he also received the right to buy $3 billion worth of common stock at any time in the next five years for just $22.25 per share. The GE deal came with the clause that the company could buy back Buffett's 10% Elite Dividends at any time for a 10% premium. It was truly a win-win for Warren and his company.

Meanwhile, common shareholders of each firm would still be down significantly on their shares. And

their dividend yields stayed below 3% even at their lows. So how did Buffett do it? In each case, he bought elite dividends.

But don't let that name fool you. You too can grab your piece of this seemingly exclusive investment market.

Here's one opportunity you can take advantage of to receive Elite Dividends...

The company is **Public Storage**. They offer a 6.5%-plus dividend yield.

Action to take: Buy shares of Public Storage Inc. 6.625% Cumulative Preferred Stock, Series Q (NYSE: PSA-Q) up to $27.08.

[NOTE: There are 17 differing series for this specific stock. Make sure you're buying the right one. Depending on what service you use, you may have to use a different ticker symbol to find this specific series. On MSN Money and Google, for example, it's PSA-Q. On Yahoo Finance, it's listed as PSA-PQ. NYSE has it listed as PSAPRQ. And E-Trade uses the symbol PSA. PR.Q. Your broker may use a different one. When investing, make sure you have the right series. To learn more about dividend investing, check out Total Income Alert *at AgoraFinancial.com.]*

Own Hassle-Free Real Estate

Mark Twain offered timeless investment advice when he wrote, "Buy land — they ain't making any more of it."

Real estate provides long-term returns through appreciation and cash yields through rent. Direct ownership also carries a tax advantage.

If you're like me, though, you probably don't have the time or desire to manage tenants, maintain the place, and deal with petty squabbles.

Luckily, there's a way to get all the advantages of investing in real estate without the hassles.

Enter **REITs**.

Certain firms hold and manage real estate properties and issue shares on stock exchanges. If they pass on at least 90% of their profits to investors, they don't pay corporate income taxes, so it works for them to pay shareholders in dividends.

Most REITs pay dividends each quarter, and some return cash to the investors each month.

REALTY INCOME (NYSE:O) Realty Income owns roughly 3,800 properties, spread out across 47 industries and in 49 states. They have a 98% occupancy rate, and most properties are rented long term. It paid out its first dividend in 1970 and hasn't missed one since. Pays a 5.4% annual yield.

INLAND REAL ESTATE CORP. (NYSE: IRC) Inland owns a $2.8 billion portfolio of shopping centers including 161 properties across the Midwest. As of writing, it has paid 116 monthly dividends since 2004. Pays 5.5% annual yield.

[NOTE: Learn more about REITs — and how to invest in them — from value investor Chris Mayer, editor of investment newsletter Capital & Crisis, *at www.agorafinancial.com.]*

Stuff Your Bank Account With Tax-Free Cash

They're called "Box 8 Dividends."

The IRS has a space for them specific type on its 1099-INT form. Right there in box 8 (hence the name). That's the box, if you don't know, for tax-exempt interest.

They're also known as municipal bonds.

With the three municipal bond funds you're about to learn about, you can earn 36 annual checks — that's three checks each and every month. Best part? Uncle Sam can't touch it!

> <u>Action to take</u>: Buy AllianceBernstein National Municipal Income Fund (AFB) up to $17.
>
> <u>Action to take</u>: Buy BlackRock Municipal Income Trust II (BLE) up to $17.63.
>
> <u>Action to take</u>: Buy Nuveen Quality Income Municipal Fund (NQU) up to $16.40 a share.

[NOTE: These three companies were originally recommended solely for Neil George's Lifetime Income Report subscribers. They're only a small part of the income-producing investments he brings to his readers week after week. For more information on Neil's income investments, visit www.agorafinancial.com.]